D1039047

ELEMENTS OF WORSHIP

Also by Judson Cornwall:

Freeway Under Construction (1974)
Give Me—Make Me (1979)
Heaven (1978)
Let God Arise (1982)
Let Us Abide (1977)
Let Us Be Holy (1978)
Let Us Draw Near (1977)
Let Us Enjoy Forgiveness (1978)
Let Us Get Together (1983)
Let Us Praise (1973)
Let Us See Jesus (1981)
Let Us Worship (1983)
Profiles of a Leader (1980)
Unfeigned Faith (1981)

With Thomas Cornwall

Please Accept Me (1979)

ELEMENTS OF WORSHIP

by
Judson Cornwall, Th.D.

Bridge Publishing, Inc.
South Plainfield, NJ 07080

Unless otherwise indicated, Scripture quotations are from *The New King James Version of the Bible*, © 1982 by Thomas Nelson, Inc., Nashville, Tennessee. Used by permission.

Scripture quotations identified MOFFATT are from *The Bible: A New Translation*, translated by James Moffatt, © 1954 by James R. Moffatt. Used by permission of Harper & Brothers Publishers, New York.

Scripture quotations identified PHILLIPS are from *The New Testament in Modern English*, translated by J.B. Phillips, © 1972 by J.B. Phillips. Used by permission of Macmillan Publishing Company, Inc.

Scripture quotations identified BERKELEY are from *The Holy Bible, The Berkeley Version in Modern English*, by Ferritt Verkuyl, © 1945 by Zondervan Publishing House.

Dedication

To Nick and Irene Welch, my children in the faith, whose lives and ministry are dedicated to bringing others into true worship.

Contents

Contents

Acknowledgments

Without the gentle encouragement and support of my wife, Eleanor Cornwall, this book would not have been written.

Without the skillful editing of my secretary, Cheryl Tipon, this book might not have been readable.

Without the constant input of my son-in-law Norbert Senftleben, who read and re-read the manuscript as it came out of my typewriter, the material presented would not have been complete.

But with their consecrated help, this book is presented to the Body of Christ. "We are God's fellow workers" (1 Corinthians 3:9).

Preface

My book *Let Us Worship*, released in 1983, has had a wide acceptance in the Body of Christ. There is a quickened awareness of the need to worship God, and that book has given guidance to many people who respond to this call of the Holy Spirit. Far from answering all of the questions that surround true worship, the book actually raised further questions in the minds of the readers.

This book seeks to answer some of those questions that have been asked of me in conferences and other public appearances. It is not a definitive book of worship, but it does explore some very practical aspects of coming into the presence of God as a worshipper. If it raises still more questions, that will prove that the book has been a thought-provoking resource on a subject that has played a minor role in far too many lives.

The standard approach to collective worship is viewed ever so briefly in the introduction, and then the book takes us to chapters five and seven of Revelation to see how worship is expressed before the Throne in heaven.

Decatur, GA
January, 1985

Introduction

Worship is one person responding in his or her spirit to the one true God, but very often this experience of worship occurs when individuals are gathered together in a collective expression to God. Actually, worship is the prime purpose for going to church on the holy day, and traditionally we have referred to the Sunday morning service as "morning worship."

While the concept of worship is older than the Church itself, all religious organizations incorporate worship as a vital part of their activities. Many of these groups, however, see worship as a noun rather than a verb—they picture worship as a pre-planned program more than as an expression of the spirit of man to the Spirit of God.

In preparing for worship, our churches have established rituals, forms, and liturgies to be used as vehicles for the expression of corporate worship. Some of these are quite elaborate; others are very simple, but all of them were developed to give some form to the public worship experience. It is accepted, of course, that

1

congregational worship needs both guidelines and guidance. As long as these programs serve the worshipper, they can be valuable, but all too frequently the ceremony substitutes for the experience, making the ritual the end instead of a means to the end.

This book is far more concerned with the elements of the worship experience itself, but it might serve a purpose to briefly consider the most common sacraments that are associated with worship in today's Church.

ELEMENTS THAT HELP TO
CREATE WORSHIP ATTITUDES

Whenever we have a gathering of people, we can also expect to have a variety of attitudes, for it is not worshippers who gather together but persons who need to be brought into worship. Anything that can be done to create an awareness of God can help the corporate worship expression.

While it certainly is not foremost, *architecture* is usually the first element that affects the attitude of the potential worshipper. Some buildings create a sense of awe, while others nearly infuse a sense of God-consciousness. I have stepped into churches that were completely empty and have almost involuntarily dropped my voice to a whisper, as though a priest or minister were functioning at the altar. I am aware that this is atmosphere—not worship—and yet the ambiance that surrounds a worshipper greatly affects him.

God is certainly aware of this, for even during the wilderness wandering of His people Israel, He provided for a costly and very ornate place of worship: the Tabernacle in the Wilderness. Much later, King

Solomon's Temple surpassed that splendor, much as a diamond surpasses the splendor of costume jewelry.

There are, of course, extreme contrasts of thought in the matter of places of worship, but whether the building has high, arched ceilings and is beautified with stained-glass windows, or whether it is nothing more than a rented storefront church, the maximum that the architecture can produce is an attitude. Still, worship is an attitude expressed, and, like it or not, our surroundings will create attitudes within us.

Ritual is another element that helps to create a worship attitude. Some Christians embrace ritual to the point of making it a substitute for worship, while others denounce it as being subversive to worship, but the truth is that all of us have some ritual in our public gatherings, and all of us have become dependent upon it. The very way a service begins becomes a ritual in most congregations, whether that ritual is a very informal greeting by the pastor, or the liturgical processional of vested priests. The fact that a method is consistently employed to inform the congregation that it is worship time makes it a ritual, and that very ritual seeks to create a corporate attitude that could lead to worship.

There are many other rituals during the course of a public worship service, all of which are intended to help a larger group of people to sense the same thing and to respond in the same way. Just as the sound of the bugle informs the troops what action is desired, so the rituals of the church can direct the congregation into united action. The ritual is, of course, just a signal for action; it can never become the action of worship.

Somewhat akin to ritual is the use of *vestments* to induce a worship attitude. The Old Testament has ample references to the vestments God provided for His priesthood, and even the prophets were frequently recognized by the garb they wore. I was raised in a religious heritage that rejected the use of vestments—I had been in the ministry for many years before we were allowed to use robes even for our choirs—and I deeply respect this rejection of vestments on the grounds that clothes cannot change the person who wears them; but I have also developed a sound respect for those who use the vestments to bring people to a worship-consciousness. The answer to abuse should not be abandonment, but historically the Church has chosen to purge rather than to purify.

I have no reason to plead for vestments, but I make the observation that to those who are accustomed to their use, they often create a visual image that enhances the worship of a congregation.

Another element used to create worship attitudes in congregations is *pageantry*. In many religious circles this very word is a decided "no-no," and yet the Old Testament feasts were full of pageantry. Whether the presentation is liturgical dancing, drama, the processional, or the lighting of candles, the symbolic representation presented for visual observation can bring people's thoughts from the world of commerce to the things of the Spirit. Of course, like a sermon that runs far too long, the theatrical aspect of pageantry can easily be overdone, but when it is presented in good taste with a sensitivity to the things of God, it can be a useful element in getting people into a worship attitude.

ELEMENTS THAT HELP
TO *DIRECT* WORSHIP ATTITUDES

With the successful creation of a sense of worship in a congregation, whatever combination of elements may have been used, it is equally imperative that the worship be directed toward a common goal. The Church has historically utilized ordinances to help guide the worship of the people. One of the best-known ordinances of the Church is the ordinance of *marriage.* Even non-church members often want a church wedding, and people will travel for miles to attend one. Marriage can be entered into with little more than a legal contract between a man and a woman, but the sacrament of marriage involves God in that union, and bringing God into the marriage can be a time of great awareness of the Divine presence.

Perhaps the second most common sacrament in our churches is *the dedication or baptism of children.* This, again, involves God in the family life of the members of the community, and it is an acknowledgment that the gift of life comes from God's hand. However the ordinance may be administered, the parents are inviting God to become involved with the raising of their child.

In a similar vein is the ordinance of *the burial of our dead.* My father, who entered the ministry when I was three years old, loved to conduct funerals. When we moved to a new community he would visit all of the mortuaries to introduce himself and to volunteer his services for any family who did not have a pastor. He told me that he never had an audience more attentive to the Gospel than the mourners in a funeral parlor, for every person who attends a funeral comes face to face with his own mortality.

Is there a time when a Christian can better demonstrate his faith than when burying a loved one? Rather than allow death to destroy our faith, the ordinance of Christian burial directs that faith to worship God in the midst of temporary sorrow in teaching that life has not been terminated—it has been transformed.

Still another ordinance that helps to direct worship attitudes is the ordinance of *baptism*. It is performed in a variety of forms, with a multitude of formulas, and even the doctrinal emphasis varies, but it is a clear command of the Word of God that can be such an affirmation of faith in and obedience to God as to lead an entire congregation into worship.

By far the most universal ordinance used to bring people into a worship experience is the ordinance of *the Lord's Supper*. It was ordained by Jesus Himself, and it has been observed in the Church from that moment until now. Many worship services are built around the serving of the Communion, and most Christians feel that in one way or another, partaking of the Communion unites them with the Lord in a life-giving way, for Jesus Himself said, " 'Most assuredly, I say to you, unless you eat the flesh of the Son of Man and drink His blood, you have no life in you. Whoever eats My flesh and drinks My blood has eternal life, and I will raise him up at the last day' " (John 6:53, 54).

ELEMENTS THAT HELP TO
RELEASE WORSHIP EXPRESSIONS

When a congregation gather together for worship, they need more than outside stimuli to inspire worship, and ordinances that help to direct that worship. They need to be allowed to release their worship in activities in which they are participants, for worship by identification is impossible; worship demands action. God did not make us mystics; we need to **do** something to make the transition from our world to His kingdom.

Singing is an essential element that enables the corporate Body of believers to release worship unitedly. Song is often the wings that lift the spirit into worship, and united singing gives support to the worship expression of others in the congregation.

Prayer is another element that enables a group of Christians to release worship unitedly. Jesus regularly used the prayer channel for times of fellowship with the Father, and Paul taught and practiced the use of prayer in worship.

Because almost all of the prayers recorded in the New Testament contain an element of doxology or praise, we can know that *praise* is an enthusiastic way for a group of people to release worship unto God, for the psalmist declared, "Enter into His gates with thanksgiving, And into His courts with praise. Be thankful unto Him, and bless His name" (Psalm 100:4). Although praise is often the vocal end of worship, it is not a substitute for worship, for praise is basically concerned with what God has done, while worship is involved with Who God is.

Confession of sin is also an element of worship, for throughout the Bible, those who came into God's presence quickly began to confess sin. It is always when we see ourselves contrasted with God's holiness and righteousness that we have our greatest awareness of sin, and the very confession of that sin is a part of our worship. It is an acknowledgment of the finished work of Christ at Calvary and a positive application of Divine grace. We should never let sin keep us out of God's presence, for confession of sin will help to bring us into His presence in a new and vital way.

In the many years that I pastored, I found that *the public reading of the Scripture* was a powerful element to bring people into a worship encounter with God. If prayer is our communication to God, the Bible is God's communication to us, and reading it aloud brings the voice of God to the minds of the entire congregation of believers, which often produces a release of worship. When God's voice is heard and heeded, the natural response of the human heart is worship.

Preaching is also an element of corporate worship. The New Testament makes great provision for preaching, since preaching declares God's Word, is a testimony of faith, enlightens, informs, and inspires people to respond to God. Anointed, Bible-centered preaching should be a part of the worship of the Church—but not a substitute for it. Preaching that exalts Christ, exposes sin, and explains redemption excites believers to worship.

ELEMENTS DARE NOT BECOME SUBSTITUTES FOR WORSHIP

Worship is the interpersonal relationship between God and man. These elements we have discussed may help a corporate body of believers to express that relationship, but by themselves they cannot produce that relationship. Each and all *may* be part of worship, but any and all of them may be performed without any actual worship transpiring. The ordinances are vehicles for worship, just as the rituals and ceremonies are aids for worship, but in themselves they are not worship. Even the congregational activities such as singing, prayer, praise, Bible reading, and preaching are not worship, either—just expressions of worship.

Ritual for ritual's sake will never produce worship. As a matter of fact, ritual often becomes the actions of our souls—our intellect and emotions. When our spirits worship, our souls get involved in expressing that worship, but soulish action rarely inspires the spirit to worship.

True worship does not require cathedrals, vestments, pipe organs, or robed choirs, but these may be elements that help to bring the saint into a worship attitude. Jesus continually emphasized that worship is a one-to-one relationship not dependent upon locale or trappings, while all the time refusing to condemn the liturgy and the Temple of His day.

The International Standard Bible Encyclopedia states this most pointedly: "Anything that really stimulates and expresses the worshipful spirit is a legitimate aid to worship, but never a substitute for it, and is harmful if it displaces it."[1]

If worship is written upon the heart of man by the hand

---

[1] *The International Standard Bible Encyclopedia*, Volume V. Grand Rapids, Michigan: William B. Eerdmans Publishing Company, 1939, page 3112.

of God and is both inseparable from life as well as being an expression of life itself, then worship should become the main occupation of each of us rather than being merely an avocation. Learning to worship should be as important as learning to walk and talk, for without worship we will never be able to lead the full and spiritually mature life for which we were created by God. It is only the true worshipper of God who has that awareness of life that escapes the scientist, eludes the politician, and evades the philosopher, but spiritual worship will not be learned from religious sacraments or forms; true worship is a person's spirit responding lovingly to an acute awareness of God. As Jesus put it, " 'God is Spirit, and those who worship Him must worship in spirit and truth' " (John 4:24).

— 1 —

Worship Is Inseparable From Life

Worship is written upon the heart of man by the hand of God. It is not culturally induced, nor is it a learned experience. It is an inherent drive as real as food-seeking or self-protection. From birth to burial, a person will be confronted with this inner craving to relate to something far higher than himself. The need to worship is inherent, but learning to properly express this craving is often complex, for there are many details that are involved in bringing man's spirit into a worship relationship with the Spirit of God. In a broad sense, worship is inseparable from life and is an expression of life. It is not that man cannot live without worship, it is that he cannot fully live without worship, so deeply ingrained in his life is this component.

If the Word of God is to be taken literally, all of creation worships God. The psalmist spoke of everything on the earth as praising God; from the sun and stars to mountains and trees, cattle and birds, kings and people, and young men and old men (*see* Psalm 148). John the revelator declared that "every creature which is in heaven and on the earth and under the earth and such as are in the sea, and all that are in them, I heard saying: 'Blessing and honor and glory and power Be to Him who sits on the throne, And to the Lamb, forever and ever!' " (Revelation 5:13).

Since all of God's creation exists for "the praise of His glory" (Ephesians 1:12), the true issue in life is not *who* will worship, but *when* and *what* they will worship! Worship is absolutely inseparable from life. Individuals and societies who have worked so hard to prevent worship have always failed, for man was made to worship as surely as he was made to breathe. We may restrict the expression of worship for a season, just as we may briefly hold our breath, but there is an inward craving for worship that cannot be permanently stilled.

WORSHIP IS UNIVERSAL

The Bible does not record a single society that did not worship, nor does the Bible deal with atheism, except for the single verse of Psalm 14:1, "The fool has said in his heart, 'There is no God.' " Aside from this occasional fool, the Bible assumes and accepts that worship is inherent in all people.

Throughout the world the spade of the archaeologist frequently uncovers ruins of various forms of temples, idols, or other memorials to the deities of ancient cultures. Often these are the most elaborate structures that are unearthed. It seems that worship was paramount in each civilization; their god was reverenced above their king. Worship, to the ancients, was central to living, and it took the highest seat of honor in their culture.

Furthermore, the recorded history of the nations of the earth fails to speak of any people who formed societies without some form of worship. Life without worship was unknown to the ancients, and it is equally unknown to modern society. We have been told for many years that explorers have never found a tribe of people, however remote or primitive, who did not worship. Worship is truly universal.

I do not imply that all peoples have worshipped God as He has revealed Himself in the Bible, for the object of worship varies from society to society, and the intensity and manner of worship differ, but everyone worships something, in some way. Some worship the sun; others worship the moon; still others choose a peculiar rock to become their god, while many carve a tree into an idol as a visible representation of their god.

Missionologists have documented that laws of worship have been taught from generation to generation among the peoples of the earth, and there is usually some form of a priesthood that oversees the worship of the society. It is truly amazing how often these laws and priesthoods seem to parallel the rituals of worship that God gave to Moses on Mount Sinai. In some way, not now fully explained, there exists a common denominator among all people of all times, and that generic force is worship. Worship is as universal to mankind as marriage is.

WORSHIP IS A CREATED INSTINCT

The final statement of the Psalter is "Let everything that has breath praise the Lord. Praise the Lord!" (Psalm 150:6). It is reminiscent of the beginning of Genesis where the creative work of God was described as "God said, 'Let there be . . .' and there was . . ." (Genesis 1:3). If God says, "Let everything praise," it is as creative as it is permissive.

Worship is not a product of education; it is a result of creation. Isolated tribes of people who never experienced communication with anyone else on earth worshipped. Man does not worship because he has learned to worship; rather, man learns to worship because an inner drive compels him to be a worshipper. Man's worship is a response to an inner instinct. He is merely doing what comes naturally. It is as normal for a person to worship as it is for him to eat.

Psychologists have identified at least eight basic drives that are inherent in each of us, and God has provided satisfaction for each drive. Every need of our bodies is met through a natural provision. Every drive of our soul finds satisfaction in something that God has provided, and each longing of man's spirit finds fulfillment in worship. Need is negated through nourishment, and God, Who created the need, also supplies the satisfaction for that need.

There is a religious cliché that is far older than you or I, but its continued existence indicates the force of the saying: "There is a God-shaped vacuum in each of us." Since God made us to have fellowship with Him, it is to be expected that when anything interrupts the flow of that fellowship, it creates a void or vacuum. There is an inner craving in man—a void—that can be satisfied and filled only by worship. Until this craving is identified, a person may try to satisfy it in many different ways. Frequently the cry of man's spirit for fellowship with God is interpreted as a physical craving for food, drink, sex, or drugs, but the "itch" in man's spirit cannot be satisfied by scratching his body or soul. Only God can fill this void.

WORSHIP IS VENERATION

If we think of the worship ingredient in purely religious terms, we will lose our awareness of how widespread and forceful it actually is. The element of worship—the raw instinct, untutored and undirected—is fundamentally an attitude of veneration, or, more properly, an expression of an inward veneration. Basically, and perhaps subconsciously, each of us has an inner awareness of our mortality. We sense our limitations and observe our repeated failures in life. All of this seems to be in conflict with the eternal portion of our being about which we know so little: our spirit. It is this eternal part of man that reaches beyond the physical, seeking contact with something higher and beyond himself. That something may be unknown, but the very inner craving for contact with it almost proves its existence. Spirit cries to spirit, or, as the Scriptures put it, "Deep calls unto deep" (Psalm 42:7).

The deep respect—the veneration—that man develops for this "something beyond himself" is forceful and motivating. Life takes on new meaning when we think we have identified this outer force or greater person. Traditionally this person has been called "god." Non-biblical concepts of "god" are as varied as the philosophies of the human races. From the mythological concepts of a god to the carved representations of demons, man has sought to impart some semblance of humanity to the gods, if for no greater reason than to be able to relate to them.

15

The veneration with which many people worship their false gods is commendable, although it is often pathetic. I have seen adults crawl great distances on their knees over cobbled streets and courtyards, tearing the flesh of their legs to shreds, in their expression of veneration to their deity. I have watched the poor bring gifts of food and money to be burned before their idol gods as an act of propitiation. Long fasts, bodily flagellations, and acts of humiliation are common expressions of reverence before heathen deities.

The great religious festivals, with their parades, partying, and revelings, are but another way of expressing an inner worship of an unknown being who is conceived as being above and beyond the mortal realm. The pagans accompanied such celebrations with human sacrifices, but modern culture has reduced this to financial sacrifice, which is, of course, more beneficial to the priesthood.

As the age of reason dawned upon Europe, science became the object of man's veneration. Idols, temples, and even churches were replaced with test tubes and laboratories. The mind of man became his god, and education became his temple. Enlightened man was expected to create a utopia on earth. The men of letters, the scientists, and the doctors became society's deities.

When industrialization became a reality in America, materialism became our new god. Wealth, and its accompanying power, were esteemed as though they were eternal. In this new world, one could worship at both the feet of science and the altar of wealth, and what homage they have received in modern history.

The objects of man's veneration are varied, but the adoration, love, inner reachings, and dedication of lives to them come from the same inner force—the desire to worship!

WORSHIP IS AMORAL

From one end to the other, the Bible severely rebukes the worship of any but the one true God, Who has revealed Himself through Jesus Christ our Lord. This condemnation, which carried with it a death penalty, does not, however, make worship immoral; it merely states that worship was used in an immoral manner.

All of the innate cravings in man are morally neutral. God created no immorality within man; God's creation of man caused Him to say that it "was very good" (Genesis 1:31). The food-seeking drive within man's nature is certainly amoral, but if it is used improperly, it can destroy man's life with poison. Similarly, man's sex drive is God-given and completely amoral, but if it is used promiscuously, it can be a destructive force rather than a constructive one.

Like these other drives, the drive to worship is amoral, but the way it is expressed and the object it chooses to venerate determine its morality or its immorality. Self-worship, which is the heart of humanism, is certainly immoral, for to make a god of ourselves falls far short of God's goal for our worship. We need God; we do not need to become a god.

Idolatry, whether it focuses on metal images or mental images, is an immoral use of worship. Materialism, sensuality, veneration of a government or of any person, whether he be an officer in government, an entertainer,

17

a sports figure, or a sex symbol, is a prostitution of our innate need to worship.

WORSHIP IS LEARNABLE

All of the natural drives that came with our births had to be trained and directed before they served us in life. Unfortunately, today's generation seems to think that the worship drive will direct itself—and it will, but it will seldom direct itself to God without some guidance.

To God, David cried, "Teach me Your way, O Lord; I will walk in Your truth; Unite my heart to fear Your name" (Psalm 86:11), and to his people he said, "Come, you children, listen to me; I will teach you the fear of the Lord" (Psalm 34:11). David was convinced that worship was both learnable and teachable.

No baby moves from feeding on the bottle to eating at the family table without outside assistance. He is shifted from formula to Pablum to strained vegetables to chopped food to adult food. He progresses from sucking to swallowing to chewing; what was once done entirely for him is done with him and eventually by him. Progressive aspects of experience and training bring the child from complete dependence to independence in satisfying his hunger drive. He learns the difference between a spoon and a nipple, and chewing and swallowing replace sucking. There is no instantaneous transfer, nor can one phase alone train him to eat with utensils, but a combination of details will do the job.

Similarly, no one detail will shift any person from immature or improper worship to the level of worship that God seeks—worship that is done in spirit and in truth (*see* John 4:23, 24). Fortunately, God is a patient and loving Father Who has shared many elements that make our worship acceptable and pleasing to Himself.

In our enlightened day, the temptation is strong to deify humanity and to worship at the throne of man's accomplishments. Since such a high percentage of what we learn is picked up by observing others, it should be profitable for us to look into God's heaven through the eyes of the apostle John and see the worship of men and angels before the Throne of God.

Worship is so forceful that it affects each life so deeply as to deny a simplistic definition. Its very complexity demands that we examine some of the ingredients, or items, that contribute to its operation, for as surely as worship is a powerful phase of our living, so there are elements that unite to produce the worship experience. The foundational principle in worship is our restored relationship to God through the vicarious intervention of Jesus Christ. He is at once the obtainer and the object of our worship.

The basic purpose of the Scriptures is to reveal to us the One Who must be the object of our worship, and to instruct us in how to direct and use our inherent capacity to worship. We are, of course, taught by both precept and parable. We are given multitudinous examples of worshippers, and we are given the songs and ceremonies that they used in worship. In the book of Revelation we are even given the very vocabulary that is used by worshippers in heaven, and their actions and expressed attitudes are recorded in sufficient detail to gently guide our own worship as we direct our veneration and adoration to the One Who, through the vicarious sacrifice of His own life, restored to man the access to God that Adam forfeited through disobedience. Without this renewed relationship, worship would be impossible.

And I saw in the right hand of Him who sat on the throne a scroll written inside and on the back, sealed with seven seals. Then I saw a strong angel proclaiming with a loud voice, "Who is worthy to open the scroll and to loose its seals?" And no one in heaven or on the earth or under the earth was able to open the scroll, or to look at it. So I wept much, because no one was found worthy to open and read the scroll, or to look at it. But one of the elders said to me, "Do not weep. Behold, the Lion of the tribe of Judah, the Root of David, has prevailed to open the scroll and to loose its seven seals." And I looked, and behold, in the midst of the throne and of the four living creatures, and in the midst of the elders, stood a Lamb as though it had been slain, having seven horns and seven eyes, which are the seven Spirits of God sent out into all the earth. Then He came and took the scroll out of the right hand of Him who sat on the throne. Now when He had taken the scroll, the four living creatures and the twenty-four elders fell down before the Lamb, each having a harp, and golden bowls full of incense, which are the prayers of the saints.

—Revelation 5:1-8

— 2 —

Worship Flows Out of Redemption

There are many elements that comprise this world of ours, and man has learned to combine these elements skillfully to form something that did not exist before. Similarly, Christians are surrounded with many spiritual elements that may be brought together to produce worship. Some of these components are inherent in the worshipper, and others are influences above and beyond himself. The very foundation of worship is an element supplied from outside the experience of man. It is an intervention of God that returns to man his rights before God, for true worship demands being in God's presence. We may praise from afar, but we worship only before the Throne of God.

The picture of worship described in Revelation 5 details at least nine elements that are involved in worship. Please read the segment of Revelation 5 that is printed on the verso page at the beginning of each chapter of this book, for everything in the chapter will be based on that portion of Scripture.

THE SCROLL IS THE FOCAL POINT
OF THE REVELATION

It would seem quite obvious, just from reading the first eight verses of Revelation 5, that the first element in worship is the scroll. Actually, this scroll is the focal point of this final portion of the Bible known as the Revelation. The first three chapters of Revelation are concerned with the Church on earth; chapter four is concerned with the Throne in heaven; but chapter five introduces a sealed book, a scroll, that seems to have inactivated heaven in some way.

It is important that we recognize that this scroll in chapter five is a scroll of redemption, not a scroll of revelation. While this sixty-sixth book of the Bible is called "The Revelation of Jesus Christ" (Revelation 1:1), the scroll seen in chapter five is found in heaven, not on earth. It is a small, sealed scroll of such magnitude and importance that every activity in heaven ceased until this scroll was opened and the provisions of its concents were met.

IT IS A SCROLL OF REDEMPTION

Some have called it the "book of creation," but creation honor was ascribed to the Lord (Revelation 4:11). Others, particularly persons in our Western culture, have described it as a scroll of revelation of end things. If Jesus were about to reveal something that had remained unknown to mankind from the beginning of time, it is far more likely that He would have been pictured as "the Word," "the Prophet, "the Teacher," or "the Apostle of our profession," but the scroll is given to a Lamb, not to a man. Since the Bible uses the Lamb as a symbol of redemption, this scroll is not so much a symbol of revelation as it is the symbol of redemption. This is further confirmed by the song which the living creatures sang: " 'You . . . have redeemed us to God' " (verse 9).

Furthermore, what followed the breaking of the seals of this scroll was not revelation of truth, but force that came against alien powers on the earth.

REDEMPTION IS FAR-REACHING

Perhaps nothing has astounded heaven more than God's provision of redemption. Angels stand amazed that fallen man is so loved by God that he has been forgiven at such a terrible price. Having never experienced redemption, heavenly beings can only theorize as to its meaning and effects. Unfortunately, many redeemed persons on the earth have a concept of redemption that is barely above the angelic understanding, for when redemption is mentioned, most of us think of the birth, life, death, and resurrection of Christ. This is good, as far as it goes, for this deals accurately with the basis of redemption; but redemption, as unveiled in the Bible, is past, present, and future. It includes all manifestations and achievements of Christ in the flesh, and it equally embraces coming revelations and more far-reaching elements than we have yet found in our redemption.

We must constantly guard against having such satisfaction in what we have in God that we lose the desire to reach for more. What we have already received is not the end; it is but a means to the end God has purposed for us in His great redemption. God has much more for His Church than we have now appropriated.

25

Everything on this earth owes its continued existence to the generous plan of redemption designed, paid for, and made available by God. Except for the intervention of God, Adam would have perished the day that he sinned, and not one human being would have been born, for all of Adam's children were born after the expulsion from the garden. It is because God approached sinning man, calling him by name, and replaced the substitute covering of fig leaves with the skin of an animal—for the vicarious shedding of blood is the key to redemption—and at that moment became the Mediator between sinful man and a holy God, that mankind was not destroyed in the garden of Eden. All persons, even the ungodly of the human race, owe whatever blessings they enjoy in life to the blood and work of Jesus Christ. Those who curse Him the most loudly, and those who reject Him ultimately, will someday find that they lived by His grace. They existed by Christ's mediatorial force, and they could have taken that into eternity, but they chose to accept it only in the parenthesis of time, so they will live without that mediatorial power throughout eternity.

In a sense, redemption is a living force that sustains the world in its grasp, preserves it from destruction, and blesses all the varied and successive generations on its surface. But all of these mediatorial mercies are as nothing when compared with what is yet to come! Redemption has its roots and foundations in the past, but its full realization is connected directly with the period and transactions to which this seven-sealed scroll speaks.

REDEMPTION IS PROGRESSIVE

That there is more to come in God's program of redemption is amply attested in the New Testament. The church in Corinth was reminded, "If in this life only we have hope in Christ, we are of all men the most pitiable" (1 Corinthians 15:19), and the young church in Rome was informed, "For we know that the whole creation groans and labors with birth pangs together until now. And not only they, but we also who have the firstfruits of the Spirit, even we ourselves groan within ourselves, eagerly waiting for the adoption, the redemption of our body" (Romans 8:22, 23).

Jesus Himself told His disciples, " 'Now when these things begin to happen, look up and lift up your heads, because your redemption draws near' " (Luke 21:28). Jesus was not implying that these devoted ones were unsaved; He was simply declaring, "The best is yet to come!"

Redemption has pledged to the saints an inheritance—a possession—but it is not yet fully redeemed, or possessed. There is a continuing work of Christ for His Church that is somehow wrapped up in this sealed scroll seen in heaven.

JEWISH LAWS OF REDEMPTION

The very word *redemption* takes its significance from provisional laws and customs of the Old Testament. At the dividing of the Promised Land following its conquest under the leadership of Joshua, God made it impossible to alienate estates beyond a given time. For an agrarian culture, land was the ultimate inheritance to be passed from generation to generation. If hard times, regardless

27

of their cause, made it necessary to sell the farm, the title could pass to the purchaser only until the year of Jubilee, which occurred every fiftieth year. In that year, all titles returned to the original owners, thus preserving God's gift for the family lineage. Consistently through the Old Testament, God's covenants and promises were given to a minimum of three generations—"to you, and your sons, and your son's sons"—but the right of inheritance was to pass perpetually down the progeny of the original possessor.

Alongside this regulation was another provision which made it the right of the nearest kin of one who had alienated his inheritance to another party, to step in and redeem it—buy it back—and retake it, at any time. This was the law of the *goel*, or kinsman-redeemer. It is beautifully demonstrated in the book of Ruth where Boaz redeemed the land that Elimelech had sold because of a famine in the land. Boaz restored this land to Naomi, the wife of Elimelech, and to Ruth, the wife of Elimelech's deceased son. Boaz went so far as to marry Ruth so that the first child would carry the family name and inheritance into Israel's future, and from that lineage Christ Jesus was born.

These two regulations gave the Jews a strong concept of redemption. There was an automatic redemption, and there was an intermediary redemption. Their property rights would be returned to them automatically in the year of Jubilee, or a kinsman-redeemer could buy back their lost estates at any time there was a combination of willingness and ability.

The terms of redemption were established at the time the property was sold. When an inheritance was sold, encumbered, or transferred away, there were two scrolls, or instruments of writing, made of the transaction. One was open; the other was sealed. The unsealed one stated the right of possession to the purchaser; basically, it was the public record of the transaction. The second scroll, however, contained both the details of the sale and the terms of redemption. This scroll had the signatures of witnesses written on the back side, and then it was rolled up and sealed. This provision is beautifully illustrated in the book of Jeremiah, when Jeremiah was instructed to be the *goel* for his uncle's son, Hanameel. He purchased Hanameel's field in Anathoth, wrote out the terms, had it witnessed, and sealed the scrolls; then God instructed him, " 'Take these deeds, both this purchase deed which is sealed and this deed which is open, and put them in an earthen vessel, that they may last many days' " (Jeremiah 32:14).

THIS SCROLL CONCERNED
A FORFEITED INHERITANCE

A sealed scroll, then, became a demonstrable sign of an alienated inheritance which could be recovered at Jubilee or through a *goel* according to the terms specified inside the sealed copy. This was well understood by the Jews in John's day. John was drawing upon common experiences from everyday life when he wrote about this sealed scroll in heaven. The Jewish mind automatically connected it with a forfeited inheritance. Someone had been forced to "sell the farm."

Most obviously, then, this sealed scroll of Revelation 5 is concerned with a forfeited inheritance. The scroll was written inside and out. Within were the specifications of the forfeiture and the terms of redemption; without were the names and attestations of the witnesses. The concept that it refers to things to be communicated is a modern prejudice based on Western thinking, not on any scriptural allusions to sealed books. We can do great violence to the Scriptures by bringing Western customs and concepts to a book written for the Eastern culture. The Eastern Jew would know, the moment you would say "sealed scroll," that it had to do with a forfeited inheritance. We Westerners think that "sealed" means that it is too confidential to be divulged, somewhat like the teachings of secret orders. But the thing that follows the breaking of the seals is not the revelation of new truth, thereby imparting hidden knowledge. What follows immediately are shouts of praise that a worthy Redeemer was found, and the subsequent chapters are concerned with the dispossessing of an enemy. A squatter is evicted!

Early in his vision of heaven, John saw a sealed scroll. If we could but read it, we would know who sold what, as well as the predetermined price of redemption.

The Scriptures record that there has been an inheritance forfeited in Eden, and the terms of this have been sealed up for many thousands of years. It is the inheritance of "all things" which God gave to His first creation, Adam. It was a high, holy, lofty, and blessed investiture, but the original possessor sinned, and it passed out of his hands to the disinheritance of all his progeny. That which God gave to Adam, and his sons, and his son's sons, and to them that were far off, was lost when Adam "sold the farm" early, before he had children. Aliens and intruders now possess what the saints on earth should possess, and from Adam's time until Revelation 5, these deeds have remained in the hand of Almighty God, with no one to take them up or dispossess the aliens. The fact that there are seven seals indicates the completeness of the forfeiture, for seven, in the book of the Revelation, is the number of completeness or perfection. This original estate is completely removed from man, apart from some competent, willing Redeemer.

THIS INHERITANCE IS HELD BY GOD

Inasmuch as the scroll is in the right hand of God, our inheritance is in the highest place of exaltation and authority in the universe. It is God Who holds the mortgage. Some people don't understand this, for they feel that when Adam sinned, he transferred to the devil everything that he had been given by God.

Let's look to the natural realm for an illustration of this spiritual principle. Let's assume that a young couple is finally able to purchase their first home. Apartment living is now behind them. They—and the bank—own a house! They understand at the outset of the purchase that making the payments will demand strict adherence to a severe budget, but it is worth it. As long as they make the mortgage payments, the house is theirs.

For months this couple maintains the necessary discipline to faithfully make the house payments. Then one day, driving home from work, the husband sees a car that seems to reach out and grab him. He stops only to check the price and to secure some information about the car, but a salesman finds it an easy task to convince this young man that he absolutely cannot live any longer without this particular car. The sight, the smell, the feel, and the ride of that car so excite his lust levels that even without discussing it with his wife, he purchases the car.

Oh, the joy of that new car! What a delightful experience it is to drive that car—until the first of the month. Now there are mortgage payments *and* car payments, with enough money to make either one, but not both of them. Since the car is the new toy, the money goes to make the car payment, and the bank gets a note explaining that the mortgage payment "will be a little late this month." When this is repeated three months in a row, the young couple receives a notice of foreclosure from the bank.

Who gets the title deed to that house? The car salesman? He is the one who tripped them up; it was his action that cost them the house. But although he caused the trouble that culminated in foreclosure, he does not get the house, for he never had a claim against that house at any time. The bank takes back the title to the house.

God gave mankind title to the earth. He explained that it was not "free and clear"; there were monthly payments to be made to help Adam, and us, to better appreciate the value of our earth. The payment was obedience, and the test of that obedience was the prohibition against the eating of the fruit of one specified tree. It was as though God said, *Adam, as long as you do not eat of the fruit of this tree, your payments are considered as made, but at whatever point you disobey and eat the fruit of the tree, I will foreclose.*

We all know the story. The first thing the devil did was to show up in the garden and "sell Adam a car." Adam's succumbing to the temptation to put his will above the will of God forced a foreclosure on the earth. Did this give title deed to the tempter? Of course not! God held the title deed, and it was He Who foreclosed on the mortgage; and in this chapter of the Revelation we see that sealed scroll in the majestic right hand of God Himself.

This is not the devil's world; it never has been; and it never will be! This is my Father's world. "The earth is the Lord's, and all its fullness, The world and those who dwell therein," David declared (Psalm 24:1). The devil is only a ursurper, a squatter, who claims to have authority on earth, and no one big enough has risen up to challenge him, not even the Church.

This title deed to the earth is in the right hand of God. No one and nothing ever takes out of the hand of God anything that gets into the hand of God. There is not enough power on earth or in hell to take this title deed out of the hand of the Almighty. As a matter of fact, John said that the problem that had inactivated heaven was the fact that "no one in heaven or on the earth or under the earth was able to open the scroll, or to look at it" (Revelation 5:3). Angels shrank back from it as beyond their qualifications. Heavenly principalities and powers stood mute and downcast as they surveyed the requirements for the work. None was able to take the scroll, for whoever took it and opened the seals had to pay the price that was written on the inside of the scroll.

Unredeemed man has consistently been unable to work out this problem of successful repossession of what was lost in Adam, even though he has tried through politics, science, arts, philosophy, and even religion. Varied and complicated have been his attempts, but all of them have resulted in disastrous failure. The lost estate of man can never be recovered by man, or angel, or spirits of the underworld.

THIS SCROLL AFFECTS
THE CHURCH ON EARTH

John wept at the sight of the unopened scroll, for, unopened, it is the Church's grief and distress. It speaks of the inheritance unredeemed—of the children still estranged from their purchased possession. John knew that if no one was found worthy, able, and willing to take it from the hand of God and break its seals, then all the promises of the prophets, and all the hopes of the saints, and all the Divine plans for a redeemed world must fail, for all of them were predicated upon man's living in and possessing his inheritance on earth.

The apostle John understood the office of the *goel* and knew that if there was failure at this point, the redemption of the purchased possession must fail. Until that scroll is opened and its seals broken, the people of God must remain in privation, sorrow, and tears. Little wonder, then, that Paul said that even creation joins humanity in groaning for redemption (*see* Romans 8:22, 23).

Yes, that scroll unopened is the Church's grief, but the scroll opened is the Church's joy and glory. It is the assertion of Her reinstatement into what Adam lost. The opened scroll is the recovery to Her of all of which She has been so long and so cruelly deprived by sin. This opened scroll is the very essence of the gospel; it is what all the ancient types prefigured. It is what the songs of the prophets foretold. This is what the first Christians and their successors were heralding over all the earth. This is what Jesus taught when He said, " 'The kingdom of heaven is at hand' " (Matthew 4:17). Jesus was declaring that what God gave to man was being restored to man because Jesus came to open the scroll and to meet all of its demands as our Kinsman-Redeemer.

THE OPENED SCROLL INSPIRED WORSHIP

It is this opened scroll that provoked, invoked, and inspired worship from heaven's inhabitants. Men and angels alike worshipped the Lamb when the seals were broken and the terms of the contract were met. Worship is difficult from the posture of slavery. When all is lost, we are given to petition and intercession, but when all is restored, we give ourselves to praise and worship. Until the redeemed become aware that the scroll of our lost inheritance has been opened, we will wail more than we will worship.

We worship not only because of personal redemption from sin but because of the restoration of our lost estate. While we correctly rejoice in our personal redemption, we must admit that this is but a small beginning of a larger end. God did not merely save lost individuals on this sin-wrecked planet we call Earth; He is saving us in an inclusive process to restore the entire earth to the Church. When the heavenly beings burst into song at the opening of the scroll, their words of worship ended with the assertion " '[You] have made us kings and priests to our God; And we shall reign on the earth' " (Revelation 5:10). They do not assert that we shall reign in heaven, but that we shall take authority on the earth. The Church has majored in "pie in the sky by and by" when She should have concerned Herself with restored authorities in the here and now. As long as we remain unaware of the redemption of our inheritance, we will continue to sing, "In the sweet by and by" while ignoring the nasty here and now.

THE INHERITANCE HAS BEEN RESTORED TO THE CHURCH "IN CHRIST"

In his glorious teaching on the resurrection from the dead, Paul affirmed that Christ was the last Adam (*see* 1 Corinthians 15:45). The Adamses are deceased, and now Christ has become the "second man" (1 Corinthians 15:47). God started all over again with mankind. The first man was placed here and given total authority over this world, but he blew it. He didn't keep up the mortgage payments. God determined to start again with a sinless man—Jesus Christ—and let Him face the temptation to disobey. Jesus was able to declare, "I do not seek My own will but the will of the Father who sent Me" (John 5:30), and at Calvary's cross He cried, "It is finished" (John 19:30). He was affirming that He had met every demand of the opened scroll. Redemption was completely paid for. All that remains is the dispossession of the squatters and repossession by the saints. God declared, "From this moment on, You are the second man. Anyone entering into the kingdom must come through birth into Your progeny."

At Calvary, God began a whole new dynasty. All who enter into this kingdom must be born of the Spirit and will have the name, nature, and inheritance of Christ Jesus. Adam's lost inheritance was restored to the Church through Christ, and we are "in Christ." Not only has relationship with God been restored, but possession and authority on earth have also been restored to the Church.

After His resurrection, Jesus made two powerful statements to His disciples. " 'All authority has been given to Me in heaven and on earth,' " He said (Matthew 28:18), and then He stated, " 'As the Father has sent Me, I also send you' " (John 20:21). Everything was restored to Christ, and He conferred that same authority upon the Church. "In My name," He said, and then He listed a line of authority that touches heaven, earth, and hell. "In My name you can do anything, because My name is Kinsman-Redeemer. I am your *Goel.* I bought it back, and now you are functioning in My name." The year of Jubilee will come when everything will again be put in our name, but at the moment, all authority is in His name, and He has shared that name with us.

As we gain an awareness of this conferred authority which comes out of a relationship with Christ, we discover that God has effected a restored relationship that has produced restored responses. We can worship because we are back in our rightful place with God. We desire to worship because the restoration was done wholly by God on our behalf. The Lion/Lamb, clothed with power and majesty, has redeemed us to God and to everything God has purposed for man to be, possess, and do.

Until we are restored to authority, to our rightful position, to our inheritance—until we come into security—it is hard for us to respond warmly to God in worship. The distance is too great for us to bridge, so God bridged it for us by restoring us to the relationship Adam had with God in the garden of Eden. From this posture we can worship. In this relationship, worship is natural. In bringing us back into Himself, God also brought us back into worship.

Little wonder, then, that the first demonstrated element in worship is the opened scroll of man's restored inheritance. It is this opened scroll that makes worship possible.

The scroll is not the object of our worship; it is the restored means to worship. Christ Jesus, Who opened that scroll, will ever remain as the center of our worship.

Now when He had taken the scroll, the four living creatures and the twenty-four elders fell down before the Lamb, each having a harp, and golden bowls full of incense, which are the prayers of the saints.

—Revelation 5:8

— 3 —

Worship Is Christ-Centered

As vital as the opened scroll is to worship, it is but one of several necessary elements that go into making up worship. A second of these worship components seen in Revelation 5 is that worship is Christ-centered—not just that worship should be, but that it *must* be, Christ-centered. When the messenger who conducted John on his tour through heaven said, " 'These are the true sayings of God,' " John "fell at his feet to worship him. But he said to me, 'See that you do not do that! I am your fellow servant, and of your brethren who have the testimony of Jesus. Worship God! For the testimony of Jesus is the spirit of prophecy' " (Revelation 19:10).

CHRIST IS THE MESSAGE OF THE BOOK

When God's Book—the Bible—is opened, Jesus is consistently revealed, for, as John was told, the spirit of prophecy is to give testimony to Jesus. He is the theme of the Bible, and He is the center of worship in the Bible. Jesus is the antitype to the Old Testament types and shadows as well as being the theme of the prophetic

41

messages. He is the subject of Bible poems and songs, and He is the object of love in all the love stories in the sacred pages. As a matter of fact, all sixty-six books of the Bible picture Jesus in one way or another.

Genesis	The Creator
Exodus	The Deliverer
Leviticus	The Scapegoat
Numbers	Cloud by Day, Fire by Night
Deuteronomy	The Prophet
Joshua	The Conquering King
Judges	The Spirit of the Lord
Ruth	The Nearest Kinsman
1 & 2 Samuel	The Anointing
1 Kings	The Chief Cornerstone
2 Kings	The Rod of Elisha
1 & 2 Chronicles	The Worthy King
Ezra	The Master Builder
Nehemiah	The Restorer
Esther	The Responsive Monarch
Job	The Daysman
Psalms	The Shepherd
Proverbs	Wisdom
Ecclesiastes	The Only Real Life
Song of Solomon	The Beloved
Isaiah	The Man of Sorrows
Jeremiah	The Potter

Lamentations .... Our Only Hope
Ezekiel .... The Promiser of Restoration
Daniel .... The Fourth Man
Hosea .... The Forsaken Husband
Joel .... The Rain
Amos .... The Plumbline
Obadiah .... God's Majestic Ruler
Jonah .... The Merciful
Micah .... The Prince of Peace
Nahum .... The Revenger
Habakkuk .... Our Strength
Zephaniah .... The Just
Haggai .... Holiness
Zechariah .... The Fountain for Sin
Malachi .... The Sun of Righteousness
Matthew .... The King
Mark .... The Servant
Luke .... The Son of Man
John .... The Son of God
Acts .... The Risen Lord
Romans .... Our Life
1 Corinthians .... Our Righteousness
2 Corinthians .... Our Source of Triumph
Galatians .... Our Substitute
Ephesians .... The Head of the Church
Philippians .... Our Example

Colossians ....Our Sustainer
1 Thessalonians .... Our Resurrecter
2 Thessalonians .... Our Returning King
1 Timothy .... Our Mediator
2 Timothy .... The Destroyer of Death
Titus.................................. The Redeemer
Philemon ....Our Benefactor
Hebrews ....The Fulfiller of the Law
James .... The Healer
1 Peter............................ The Living Stone
2 Peter............................... The Renovator
1, 2, 3 John ....God's Manifest Love
Jude......................................The Presenter
Revelation......................... The Lion/Lamb

Every book of the Bible pictures Jesus, and if we do not see Him, we have not rightly discerned the Word of truth.

CHRIST JESUS IS THE CENTER OF OUR WORSHIP

At whatever point we turn from the testimony of Jesus, our worship becomes warped, for Jesus is both the message of the Book and the center of our worship. It is, of course, His Person, not His performance, that becomes the object of our worship. Because our knowledge of what Christ has done is better than our actual knowledge of Him, we often get caught up in His works rather than in His wonderful Person. Here in Revelation it was not the opening of the seals of the scroll that produced worship—for this merely made worship possible—but it was the presence of the Lion/Lamb, the worthy One, that produced the worship. Thanksgiving and praise are often responses to Christ's deeds, but worship is always based on His Person. Fundamentally, worship is a person responding to a person, so we can't worship until we get a glimpse of God. We can praise out of our memory circuits, but we must worship out of a present relationship; that is, we must be in God's presence to worship. True worship will not begin to flow until we get a good glimpse of Christ Jesus.

WE WORSHIP THE KING, NOT HIS KINGDOM

In the passage before us, Christ is seen as the Lamb of God, and He is worshipped as the Lamb, not as the King. We serve in God's kingdom here on earth, and we actually play an important part in establishing that kingdom on the earth, but it is the King—not the kingdom—that becomes the object of our affections.

Undue response to position or power in the kingdom of God will hinder, not help, our worship of the King of kings. Remember the disciples who squabbled over their positions of power and greatness in the coming kingdom? They were not worshipping; they were lusting. It has not changed in our generation. Those who are concerned with personal power or recognition of their spiritual gift are not worshippers; they are ladder-climbers.

When Jesus was on this earth, the religious leaders who yearned for an earthly kingdom never worshipped Him. They crucified Him. How we need to guard against a lusting for power, position, or recognition, because it will destroy worship in us.

45

This is not to deny that God has shared authority and position with us here on the earth. We all have our place in His kingdom. There are differences in offices, varieties of giftings, and pluralities of ministries, but when it is worship time, who cares! It is not the position from which we worship that matters— it is the Person we worship Who must occupy our full attention.

Many times, as the guest speaker at a church conference, I turn to the conference director and say, "It looks to me as if we have about fifteen pastors present today."

"How would you know?" the director asks. "You've never been in this area before."

"They're easy to spot," I answer. "Look at the men who have folded their arms and are looking all around. They are so used to being worshipped by their congregations that they cannot bring themselves to be the worshippers."

The tragedy of this attitude is that the Bible consistently teaches that the triune God is the only acceptable object of worship. All other worship is classified as idolatry.

On two separate occasions, the apostle John fell to worship his conducting messenger, and both times he was told, " 'Worship God!' " (Revelation 19:10, 22:8). How pastors need to communicate this to their congregations. They need to cry out, "Don't worship me! I'm a person just like you. Let's worship God together!" This would never lessen the authority of the pastor; it would actually amplify it in the eyes of the members of the congregation.

SEEING JESUS AS GOD INSPIRES WORSHIP

The disciples did not worship the Jesus with Whom they traveled until He was unveiled to them as the Christ of God. The woman at the well actually entered into an argument with Jesus until He revealed Himself to be the Messiah, and then she became an instant worshipper and a missionary-evangelist. After the Resurrection, Mary thought that Jesus was the gardener, and she pled with Him for information as to where the body of Jesus had been transferred; but the moment Jesus revealed Himself to her as the risen Lord, she worshipped Him.

The message of the early church was " 'God has made this Jesus, whom you crucified, both Lord and Christ' " (Acts 2:36), and where this message was received and believed, people worshipped.

Where there is an awareness of Christ's presence and position, there is an automatic response of worship unless something is done to repress it, for we were created to worship. To prevent worship, it is necessary to repress this created instinct, and too often religion stifles, rather than kindles, worship responses.

In our picture of worship in Revelation, after the innumerable company of the redeemed offer praise to God and to the Lamb, we read, "And all the angels stood around the throne and the elders and the four living creatures, and fell on their faces before the throne and worshiped God" (Revelation 7:11). A little later we find these words: " 'Fear God and give glory to Him . . . and worship Him who made heaven and earth, the sea and springs of water' " (Revelation 14:7). So even in eternity, the triune God will be the only object of our worship.

47

CHRIST JESUS IS THE
CAUSE OF OUR WORSHIP

In the book of Hebrews there is an interesting verse that says, "Looking unto Jesus, the author and finisher of our faith" (Hebrews 12:2). Here "faith" speaks of the inclusive concepts of God that have been committed to us through the Scriptures. Worship is the heart of those concepts. The Berkeley translation of the New Testament puts it this way: "Looking unto Jesus, the cause and completor of our faith." He is the cause and completor not only of our codified faith, but also of our response to that faith in worship of God. Christ Jesus is actually the *cause* of our worship.

We are accurate in referring to Christ Jesus as the cause of our worship, for He redeemed us back to God, making worship possible. The work of the cross was far more than a rescue from sin and hell. The evangelical emphasis upon this is truth, but it is not the full truth, and partial truth often limits us from seeing the whole truth. Salvation from sin is only a step in a larger process. The ultimate purpose of Christ's coming was to restore us to a loving relationship with the Father. There are progressive steps in returning us to this pre-fall relationship, and all of them are part of God's great salvation.

It takes very little Bible knowledge to understand that the sinful cannot stand in the presence of a holy God. In the Old Testament, even the appearance of a holy angel, who is but a messenger of God, caused the unholy to collapse in fear, expecting instant death. If the presence of a mere angel produced such fear, how could an unsanctified man stand in the presence of the holy God of heaven? Holiness is the essential nature of God—He is more holy than He is all His other attributes put together—but carnality is the essential nature of unredeemed persons.

Two conflicting realities confront us. God is ultimately holy, and He desires to bring us, the unholy, into His presence as worshippers. To reconcile the differences in these desires, God makes His holy nature available to us in Christ. Paul explained it thus: "But of Him you are in Christ Jesus, who became for us wisdom from God—and righteousness and sanctification and redemption—that, as it is written, 'He who glories, let him glory in the Lord' " (1 Corinthians 1:30, 31). Christ is our sanctification! He has been made holiness to those who are "in Christ Jesus."

The quotation from the Old Testament used by Peter is less a command and more a commitment: " 'Be holy, for I am holy' " (1 Peter 1:16). Knowing man's inability to produce holiness, God has provided that our intimate relationship with Christ Jesus will effect an infusion of the Divine nature into our lives. When we are in the presence of our holy God, we are changed "from glory to glory" (*see* 2 Corinthians 3:18).

If the unholy cannot stand in God's presence, then we cannot expect the unholy to worship, because worship requires being in God's presence. Hence Christ is the cause of our worship, since He is both the revealer of the Father and the channel whereby God's holiness is transferred into our natures.

CHRIST HAS BECOME OUR BRIDEGROOM

In every one of the ten basic Bible divisions, our relationship to God is depicted, declared, or demonstrated to be that of husband-wife, or bride-bridegroom. Christ is the Husband, and the Church is His Bride. From the Genesis account of Isaac and Rebekah, to the propetic cry " 'Return, O backsliding children,' says the Lord; 'for I am married to you' " (Jeremiah 3:14), through Paul's declaration "For I am jealous for you with godly jealousy. For I have betrothed you to one husband, that I may present you as a chaste virgin to Christ" (2 Corinthians 11:2), culminating in the invitation " 'Come, I will show you the bride, the Lamb's wife' " (Revelation 21:9), God's Word has chosen the most common of intimate relationships in life to illustrate the closeness of interpersonal involvement that has been restored to the Church here on earth.

By becoming the Bridegroom to the Church, Christ Jesus has brought a sweet, glorious intimacy back to the believers, so that we can have a need-meeting relationship with Him.

The creation of Eve illustrates this relationship. Adam was made in the image of God for fellowship with God. God desired a love object and used Himself as a model. He even imparted the breath of His life to make man a living soul. It was as though God had a baby. The fellowship in the garden of Eden met God's needs completely, but Adam's needs were not completely satisfied, for it was God, not Adam, Who declared, " 'It is not good that man should be alone; I will make him a helper comparable to him' " (Genesis 2:18). In the subsequent action, God did for Adam very much as He had done for Himself. He took a part out of Adam and formed it into a distinctly separate body, and then informed Adam that if he desired to be as complete as he used to be, he would have to relate to the other half of him. God made a love object for Adam that was more than an optional arrangement, for, to be complete, each needed the other person. Marriage brings two incomplete persons together to complete each other. Some speak of this as two halves coming together to form one whole, while others prefer to think of it as two incomplete entities so interacting as to assist each other to become a complete person.

However marriage may be illustrated, the creation story seems to list at least four reasons for marriage. First, it is God's answer to loneliness. Second, it is a need-meeter, for what one partner lacks, the other supplies, and vice versa. The third reason for the creation of Eve was to provide for man a helper who was comparable to him. Marriage is a team of equals— different, but equal. Different does not mean inferior; it simply means different. The fourth reason for marriage was procreation.

Through marriage, God has placed us in a daily relationship that consistently pictures what He wants from us as "the Lamb's wife." He wants us to be so eager to meet His needs (while He is equally eager to meet our needs) that we become helpers, or co-laborers, inter-acting one with the other. Through Christ Jesus, God has given us His name, His nature, and His authority. In a sense, then, He has made us helpers "comparable" to Himself.

51

LOVING SAINTS SATISFY
THE HEART OF GOD

In worship, saints interact with God not to get, but to give; not to have their needs met, but to meet the needs of God. Worship causes the worshipper to be more interested in the fellowship than in what may come out of that fellowship.

For many years we have been told of the God-shaped vacuum that is in the life of every person, and that none can be fully satisfied until that vacuum is filled with God. This is, of course, illustratively true. But how about the man-shaped vacuum in the heart of God? If God took part of Himself out to form man, it left a vacuum that only man can fill. When man returns to the heart of God in love—no longer as a child, but as a bride—it satisfies, completes, and fulfills God. Without getting into all the deep theological implications that God cannot have a need if He is a self-sufficient God, let us understand that when we start dealing with the emotion of love, we uncover needs, for it is impossible to have love without having needs. The first need of love is to find an object upon which to lavish that love, and the next need is to have that love returned. God did the first in creating man; now He longs, with deep need, for the love object to return that love back to its source: God.

Just as the motivational force and channel of expression in marriage is love, so worship is fundamentally love responding to love; or, better yet, worship is two lovers responding to each other.

CHRIST JESUS IS THE COMPLETOR
OF OUR WORSHIP

As the Bridegroom, Christ is the cause—the originator —of our worship. The initiative is His. We cannot worship until we are in His presence. But our verse in Hebrews (2:12) says that Christ is both the cause and the completor of our worship.

As a guest in the home of a young pastor on a particular occasion, I borrowed his study to use his computer for a few moments. He walked in and asked, "Brother Cornwall, have you ever paid any attention to the Moffatt translation of Psalm 45:10, 11?"

I had to admit that although I had read that translation through some years ago, I did not remember that particular passage. So he turned to it and read, "Listen, O bride, and bend your ear! Forget your own folk and your father's house; and when the king desires your beauty, yield to him—he is your Lord." Immediately this became my favorite translation of this passage.

It seems to me that most worshippers desire the King's beauty. Their approach to God is based on their personal needs. Their worship is an expression of their desires, but the Scriptures teach exactly the opposite to this. They teach that worship is responding to the King's desire for our beauty. Worship is presenting ourselves to meet the needs of our living God, Who has expressed an interest in love.

When Gabriel informed Mary that she had been chosen to mother the Messiah, she replied, according to the Phillips translation, " 'I belong to the Lord, body and soul; let it happen as you say' " (Luke 1:38). This is the attitude that God wants from the hearts of His

53

worshippers. We need to recognize that Christ Jesus is not only the cause of our worship, because of the marriage relationship, but He is the completor of our worship as well. True worship is a willingness to respond to the Bridegroom's desires. It is submission to meet His needs. It is a response to His wooings and expressions of love.

Men often have difficulty worshipping because they see this as a feminine role. "How can I be the Bride of Christ?" men ask, but it should be no more difficult for men to see themselves as the Bride of Christ than it is for women to accept the image of being a "son of God." In Christ Jesus there is neither male nor female, Paul said (*see* Galatians 3:28).

SUBMISSION IS A KEY TO WORSHIP

In the Bible, God is always pictured as the Husband, and we are always the Bride. Worship is far more a response to God's desires than an expression of our own desires, so *submission*, rather than *aggression*, is the key to worship. Actually, when we get overly aggressive in worship, we risk destroying the worship experience, for we don't lead God in worship—He leads us. God can set the mood and the tempo of worship perfectly. He's a great Lover. Worship actually becomes a relaxed response to God's expressions of love when we allow Him to be dominant.

We can get so involved in *doing* worship that there is no worship. Most of what we loosely call worship isn't worship. At the highest possible level it is a channel through which worship can flow. True worship is a response to a Person, not a religious performance. Worship is recognizing that the King desires our beauty.

If our response is to come into His presence to be loved and to love, then we enter into a worship experience. Worship is enjoying God, not working for Him.

In the Old Testament, God prohibited His priests from wearing anything that would cause sweat when they came into the Holy Place to minister unto Him. Worship must remain a "no sweat" activity. Don't work at it; yield to it. When we learn to relax in the presence of God and to enjoy Him completely, we will discover that He is actually enjoying us as well.

SEEING JESUS IS THE
FIRST STEP IN WORSHIP

The request of the small group of Greeks that came to Philip needs to be the cry of our church congregations: " 'Sir, we wish to see Jesus' " (John 12:21). Worship leaders need to hear this cry ringing in their ears. The people do not need to see the leader, nor do they need to be dazzled by the talent of the musicians. They don't even need to know everything that the leader knows about the Bible. They need to see Jesus, for to behold Him is to love Him, and to love Him is to worship Him.

We need to see Jesus because this transfers attention from ourselves to Himself, and self-centeredness must surrender to Christ-centeredness if there is to be true worship. It has been my experience that worship without an awareness of Christ is impossible, for the greater our awareness of anything other than Christ, the weaker our worship will be.

Undue consciousness of our surroundings or of the style of worship will pull our attention from Christ back to ourselves. Frequently I am on a church platform during worship time. The TV lights and cameras are trained on me, and I am facing several hundred people. I find my mind moving from a Christ-consciousness to a self-consciousness as I wonder if my tie is straight, if my shirttail has come out, or if my coat is hanging correctly. At other times my mind wanders from worship to the book chapter I happen to be writing at the time. In all such occurrences, worship, for me, ceases, for I cannot look at myself and worship God.

When Christ, as God's Lamb, stepped into the midst of these living creatures and the elders, they "fell before Him." They worshipped from a subservient position. Worshippers must always take a place lower than that of the One Who is worshipped. Human pride must melt, for worship out of pride is impossible.

How do we deal with human pride? How do we overcome religious pride? It will be quite automatic when we enter into a proper relationship with Christ. As we keep Him focused in our attention, we will find ourselves flowing out our love to Him rather than focusing on our love of ourselves, for we will recognize His worthiness to be worshipped.

And they sang a new song, saying: "You are worthy to take the scroll, And to open its seals; for You were slain, And have redeemed us to God by Your blood Out of every tribe and tongue and people and nation, And have made us kings and priests to our God; And we shall reign on the earth."

—Revelation 5:9, 10

— 4 —

Worship Recognizes
Christ's Worthiness

It is certainly not by accident that among the songs and choruses that we sing together are many that eulogize and extol the worthiness of the Lord Jesus, for recognizing His worthiness is another essential element in worship. The sacred account records that the residents of heaven acclaim this worthiness again and again. They are not establishing that worthiness; they are simply extolling it as part of their expression of worship.

We do similarly in singing "Thou Art Worthy," or "Worthy are you, Lord," or "Worthy is the Lamb that was slain." Whether we fully understand what is meant by Christ being worthy, or whether we say it because it is a scriptural expression, the Spirit within us responds in a most positive way, reinforcing whatever inner attitude we may have concerning Christ's worthiness. Since the Holy Spirit is actually leading us into worship, He even helps select the vocabulary that best expresses what should be said; and "Thou art worthy, O Lord" is very high in this vocabulary of worship.

IS WORTHY TO BE WORSHIPPED

highly improbable that any Christian would
the certainty that Christ is worthy to be
worshipped, for this is an accepted fact among all
believers. It is equally an accepted reality in the heavens,
but in heaven this truth is stated over and over again as
though something is gained in the very act of repeating it
aloud. Four times in this one chapter the word "worthy"
is used of our Lord Jesus Christ, for this chapter
establishes Christ's right to be worshipped. Until now it
has been the "Lord God Almighty" (Revelation 4:8) Who
was the object of worship, but here, in chapter five, it is
the "Lion of Judah," the "Root of David," the slain
"Lamb" Who receives the worship of heaven's mighty
ones.

John declared that in heaven, Jesus Christ of Nazareth
is worshipped as the Lord God Almighty. To us this is
academic, but to the early Church this was the
controversy that induced such extreme persecution, for
the concept of the Trinity was unknown to Judaism.
Their hallmark was " 'Hear, O Israel: The Lord our God,
the Lord is one!' " (Deuteronomy 6:4), and the worship of
anyone or anything short of God was seen as idolatry.

It was Christ's acceptance of worship that so infuriated
the Jews, and the Christians who insisted upon
worshipping this Jesus following His death and
resurrection were viewed as heretics involved in idolatry.
This motivated Saul of Tarsus to campaign against this
sect with such physical fury as to kill, maim, imprison,
and intimidate the Christians. His subsequent conversion
to Christ and his energetic preaching that Christ Jesus
was very God of very God so stirred the animosity of the

Jews against him that he was persecuted wherever he went in the world. The issue was really not doctrine; it was the declaration that Christ was God, and therefore Christ was worthy to be worshipped by word, action, and life.

Both Paul and John pointed to the death, burial, and resurrection of Christ as attestations of His divinity. This fifth chapter of the book of Revelation is based upon the vicariousness of Christ's death, for John called Him the "Lamb slain" (verse 6), quoted the elders as saying, " 'You were slain, And have redeemed us to God by Your blood' " (verse 9), and recorded that the angels chanted, " 'Worthy is the Lamb who was slain' " (verse 12). Heaven's residents proclaim that Christ's death gave Him the right to be worshipped, since that death was vicarious, substitutionary, and atoning. Furthermore, the book of Revelation declares that it is the shed blood of Jesus Christ, our Redeemer, that gives us a right to worship, for without redemption there could be no worship. It is the restoration of man's lost estate and position that has returned us to worship, and it is fitting that we worship the One Who restored us to the position of worshippers.

In Paul's doctrinal declaration of Christ's worthiness to receive our worship, he wrote, "Therefore God also has highly exalted Him and given Him the name which is above every name, that at the name of Jesus every knee should bow, of those in heaven, and of those on earth, and of those under the earth, and that every tongue should confess that Jesus Christ is Lord, to the glory of God the Father" (Philippians 2:9-11). Harmonious with this, John heard the great heavenly beings cry out, " 'Worthy is the Lamb who was slain To receive power and riches and wisdom, And strength and honor and glory and blessing!' " (Revelation 5:12). Furthermore, John observed that all of creation places Jesus and Almighty God on an equal level in the matter of worship, for he wrote, "And every creature which is in heaven and on the earth and under the earth and such as are in the sea, and all that are in them, I heard saying: 'Blessing and honor and glory and power Be to Him who sits on the throne, And to the Lamb, forever and ever!' " (verse 13). In heaven the four living creatures worship Jesus, the twenty-four elders worship Jesus, the angels worship Jesus, and all creation gives worship to Him. He is, indeed, worthy to be worshipped!

The Almighty God Who was seen in unity in the Old Testament is revealed in Trinity in the New Testament, and this glimpse into heaven given here in this final book of the Bible shows worship flowing to God the Father, God the Son, and God the Holy Spirit without partiality or jealousy. The cry of the Old Testament is unchanged— "The Lord our God, the Lord is one!"—but our concept of God is greatly enlarged in the New Testament, for "the Word became flesh and dwelt among us, and we beheld His glory, the glory as of the only begotten of the Father, full of grace and truth" (John 1:14). This increased revelation enlarged our capacity to worship, and it made our relationship to God far more intimate. Through the work of Christ, God has been revealed as loving and approachable, making worship pleasurable and personal.

CHRIST'S WORTHINESS INSPIRES WORSHIP

Each of the four times the word "worthy" is used of the Lord Jesus Christ in this fifth chapter of Revelation, the Greek word used is *axion*, which the scholars tell us means "worthy by rank and character as well as by ability." It is closely related to the word *hikanos*, which means "capable or qualified." John comfortably established that Christ is worthy of worship by virtue of His rank, character, ability, and actions. None is more qualified to receive worship from the saints on earth and in heaven than our Lord Jesus Christ.

That Christ is worthy of worship by virtue of His **rank** is self-evident. In this chapter, John listed five separate positions held by Christ, any one of which makes Him worthy of our worship. In verse 5 He is the "Lion of the tribe of Judah"—the *Conqueror.* In this same verse He is titled the "Root of David"—the *King.* In verses 6, 8, and 12 Christ is called the "Lamb of God"—the *Savior;* in verse 9 He is the "Redeemer"—the *Kinsman-Redeemer.* The fifth rank that John listed as appropriate for Jesus is the "One who sits on the throne"—the *eternal Son of God.* If there were no other reason to inspire our worship of Jesus, this five-fold rank should make us worshippers, much as five stars on the shoulders of a man in an Army uniform will bring immediate salutes from enlisted men, even if they know nothing about him.

Christ is equally worthy of worship by virtue of His **character.** Military personnel will testify to occasions when they saluted the uniform rather than the man wearing the uniform, for they found the character of the officer to be below dignity, but the office he held was worthy of the respect of a salute nonetheless. This can never be said of the Lord Jesus, for His rank and His character are beautifully matched. As the "Lion of the tribe of Judah," He is strong, forceful, powerful, and unconquerable. He is not merely a forceful Lion—the king of the jungle—but He is the "Lion of the tribe of Judah," exercising His power and authority on behalf of His people. None dares resist Him. None takes prey out of His hand. No one can stand in the day of His wrath, for He is invincible on behalf of His Church on the earth.

As the "Root of David," He is King eternal—the promised heir Who would perpetually sit upon David's throne. All dominion, authority, power, and might have been delivered into His hands, and He exercises His kingly role for the benefit of His subjects. On earth we are accustomed to seeing that ultimate power corrupts ultimately, but in the Lord Jesus we see that ultimate power controls ultimately. No matter what earthly rulers do, Christ still rules and overrules on behalf of His Church.

As the "Lamb of God," Jesus is the vicarious sacrifice, meek, lowly, unthreatening, available, and lovable to His saints. The Gospel accounts of the arrest and crucifixion of Christ emphasize the lamb-like nature He exhibited during His ordeal. The prophet Isaiah wrote, "He was led as a lamb to the slaughter, And as a sheep before its shearers is silent, So He opened not His mouth" (Isaiah 53:7). Never once was the threatening roar of the Lion heard when the role He was to fill was that of the sacrificial Lamb.

The character of Christ as the "Kinsman-Redeemer" is revealed when we see Him willing to empty Himself of all His Divine prerogatives and take on our humanity so that He would be the nearest relative to each of us. Although He became man, He never ceased being God, so He was sufficiently wealthy or able to pay the required price to redeem everything for us. His character is also revealed in His being ultimately willing and unselfishly generous in executing the office of the *goel.*

Viewed as the One "who sits on the throne," Christ is seen as eternal God, equal with the Father, having all power and authority in heaven and on the earth. Surely, then, He is completely worthy of our worship by virtue of His character in the various offices He fills.

The Greek word *axion*—"worthy"—also speaks of being worthy by virtue of **ability.** On this account alone Christ would be declared worthy of worship, for none in his wildest imagination could conceive of anything beyond the scope of Christ's ability. Jesus Himself said, " 'All authority has been given to Me in heaven and on earth' " (Matthew 28:18). John had already established Christ's activity in creation, for he wrote, "All things were made through Him, and without Him nothing was made that was made" (John 1:3), and "For You created all things" (Revelation 4:11).

Furthermore, Christ alone was able to take the scroll from the hand of the Father, open it, and fulfill its requirements. Having done this, Christ " '. . . redeemed us to God' " (verse 9), " '. . . made us kings and priests to our God' " (verse 10), and received the commitment of all " 'blessing and honor and glory and power . . . forever and ever' " (verse 13). He not only has unlimited ability; He has used that ability in a most honorable and praiseworthy manner.

RECOGNIZING CHRIST'S WORTHINESS IS WORSHIP!

Again and again as we hear heaven's inhabitants vocalizing the worthiness of Christ, we become aware that the very recognition of that worthiness is an act of worship. It is homage paid, reverence given, and admiration expressed.

Perhaps those in heaven have comfortably come into a recognition of two things that are essential to worship, while we on the earth grapple with them constantly. First of all, worship demands recognition that *all things come from God.* John said so in writing, " 'You are worthy, O Lord, To receive glory and honor and power; For You created all things' " (Revelation 4:11). As the specific Creator of all things, God is the ultimate Owner of everything. None of us is a true "owner" of anything; we are merely trustees of a few things that Christ has granted us to use. Paul quoted the psalmist in saying, "The earth is the Lord's, and all its fullness" (1 Corinthians 10:26, 28). Worship is more than just giving God "His share of the crop" by paying the tithe; it is acknowledging that the entire crop is His, and that He has allowed us to participate in it. In short, bowing in worship is an acknowledgment of our complete subservience to and dependence upon God, Who is the Proprietor of all things.

The second recognition worship demands is that *all things must return to God.* Following his statement that God had created all things, John added, ". . . and for thy pleasure they are and were created" (Revelation 4:11, KJV). In speaking through the prophet, God said, " 'Everyone who is called by My name, Whom I have created for My glory; I have formed him, yes, I have made him' " (Isaiah 43:7), and the wise man declared, "The Lord has made all things for Himself" (Proverbs 16:4). Creation does not exist for man; it exists by and for the will of God. Even man, the highest of all creation, exists by and for the will of God. Not only does nothing on this earth truly belong to us, but we ourselves belong to God by right of His creation and subsequent redemption. A true worshipper must learn to sing from deep in his inner being:

> I'm not my own—I'm Yours;
> I'm not my own—I'm Yours;
> Bought with the blood of Jesus,
> I'm not my own—I'm Yours.

The essential and simple meaning of the Hebrew word for worship—*shachah*—is "to prostrate." Worship is that attitude of life which takes the low place of absolute reverence in the presence of the Giver and Sustainer of all life. Worship is an attitude which recognizes superiority and our dependence upon the benevolence of that superior One. Worship is a word full of force, which constrains and compels us to adopt the attitude of reverence.

RESPONDING TO CHRIST'S WORTHINESS IS WORSHIP

The word "worship" runs through the entire Bible, and the thought of worship is found from Genesis to Revelation. Worship, in the Bible, has its beginnings in a three-fold acknowledgment by man: (1) The sufficiency in Christ; (2) our dependence upon Christ; and (3) our completion through Christ. When we concede the Divine sufficiency and our absolute dependence upon that Divine sufficiency, and can confess that all we need in our own lives can be found in the life of God, we are beginning to worship, for we worship in the presence of God when we acknowledge that in Him we find everything our lives demand. We become worshippers as we discover that in ourselves we are incomplete everywhere except when we are brought into relationship with Him. Since Christ Jesus has become our source of everything we receive from God, He is, indeed, worthy to be worshipped by each of us.

Although the word "worship" runs throughout the Bible, it is not specifically defined anywhere therein, but is illustrated profusely. The overriding principle behind worship seems to be a sense of individual need and God's resource to meet that need. It is an awareness that life finds only its highest and its best, and fulfills itself in relation to Him, that produces the attitude and act of worship.

While worship is far more than an attitude—it is actually an attitude expressed meaningfully—any attempt at worship that does not flow out of a correct attitude will be abortive. While the attitude of worship may be a little nebulous, it can be illustrated from experiences in life with which we are familiar. For instance, the attitude of worship is the attitude of a subject bent before the king. It is an attitude of subservience, homage, reverence, and obedience. It recognizes that life and death lie in the authority that our King represents.

We might further illustrate the attitude of worship by

watching a child yield all its love to its father. Arms are locked around father's neck, and legs hug his waist. The response to the father's expressed love is to effectively flow into the father. The hugs and kisses are an expression of complete surrender to the father. The child is aware of absolute dependence upon the father, but at the moment the one ambition is to adequately exhibit love to daddy. When saints can respond to God's love without inhibition, they are becoming worshippers.

Perhaps the zenith of worship is realized in the use of two words which translators worldwide have chosen to transliterate rather than to translate, so no matter where you may be in the world, these words will be the same. They are "Amen" and "Hallelujah." Both of these words pack an emotional punch in expressing our worship unto God.

The lexicographers define "amen" this way: "Used especially at the end of prayers to express solemn ratification or approval" (*Merriam-Webster Dictionary*). That is the way it seems to be used in Revelation 5:14; following the prayers of every creature in heaven and on the earth, ". . . the four living creatures said, 'Amen!' " It was a voiced approval of a united prayer. But in Revelation 7:12, heaven's worshippers began the prayer with the "Amen!" as though their approval was being given to God rather than to what they were saying. Actually, this is the biblical use of "Amen"—it is an expressed approbation of the will of God.

If the book of Revelation were being written today, I wonder if perhaps John would use our word "okay." Isn't the attitude of worship the attitude of saying "okay" to God in everything?

"I see in Your Word what You want, God. Okay!"

"That's where we're going? Okay!"

"You need me to work with You? Okay!"

True worshippers will not seek to impose their wills upon God, but they find a nearly automatic response within their hearts—Amen! Worshippers are like lovers—eager to surrender to the object of their love; and to worshippers of God, the word "amen" is their expression of that submission. Our love for Him is proved in our bowing to His expressed desires. Amen!

The second descriptive word that is so valuable in times of worship is "Hallelujah!" Its literal meaning is "Hallel to Jehovah." Some years ago when I was in Jerusalem as a convention speaker, I sat in a committee meeting in a basement room of a large hotel. The sound of singing, dancing, happy voices, and musical instruments filtered through the wall from the adjoining room, I turned to the Arab pastor seated next to me and asked, "What's going on next door?"

He replied, "They're having a hallel."

"Oh," I answered, in a tone indicating I did not understand.

"You don't understand the word 'hallel'?" he asked. "There has been a wedding, and friends of the bride and groom are celebrating together with a big party."

"We call that a wedding reception," I told him.

If "hallel" is a celebration, and "Ja" is but a contraction for Jehovah, then "Hallelujah" means a celebration of God! Worship is more than saying "okay" to God's desires; it is actually celebrating God Himself. The method of celebration may take varied forms, but the attitude of celebration remains constant. Whether we see ourselves as the bride or merely as friends of the bridegroom, worship is an entering into the festivities of the presence of God.

Actually, worship is a balance between the attitude of dependence on the one hand and celebration on the other. There is always the underlying consciousness that everything we need is in God, and that the measure of our abandonment to Him (amen, okay) determines the level at which our need will be met. Upon this foundation, our spirits rise in expressions of praise, adoration, jubilation, and joy. With such a foundation for worship, our very lives become a song, a psalm, an anthem—the music that glorifies God. We become a worship unto God.

If, as I have suggested, worship is an attitude of life rather than a mere expression of a passing emotion, then the outward acts are the least important parts of our worship. If we have not been worshipping God during the week, it is improbable that we will worship Him on Sunday, for if there has been no song unto the Lord for six days, we are not prepared to sing His praise on the seventh. Worship flows from a worshipper whether he is in church or at the office, for Christ is worthy to be worshipped anywhere, at any time. Christ's worthiness is constant, and where our attitude of dependence and celebration remain constant, Christ is worshipped in the very way we live.

OBEDIENCE TO GOD'S LAW IS WORSHIP

Some expressions of worship become very ornate in the surroundings of magnificent architecture, beautiful vestments, voiced pipe organs, and robed choirs, but unless that worship flows out of a life surrendered

71

completely to the will of God, it will never reach the inner sanctuary to glorify God. Christ is worthy of the worship of submitted lives as well as of spoken and sung praises, but one cannot substitute for the other; they are like the two wings of a bird that work together making flight possible.

Just as creation worships God by functioning within the realm of God's law for it, so a person worships when he is what God meant him to be. Paul wrote, ". . . that we who first trusted in Christ should be to the praise of His glory" (Ephesians 1:12). It is conceivable that a person may sing every song in the hymnbook, but never worship; may recite every creed that was ever written, but never worship; may kneel in long prayers or fast often, but still never worship. The song, the sacrifice, and the prayer are nothing unless the individual has surrendered to what God meant him or her to be. I have found that when I am what God intended me to be, my whole life worships God. It cannot be worship of God to go to Africa as a missionary if the will of God is for a person to stay home and work in commerce. Sacrifice *for* Christ is not necessarily worship, but submission *to* Christ is worship!

In a very real sense, worship consists of the finding of my own life and the yielding of it totally to God for the fulfillment of His purpose. Worship is discovering God's law, answering that law with life, and walking in the way of His appointing. It is allowing our Creator to direct every facet of our lives to the fulfillment of His purposes. Just as the angels worship God both by homage expressed and by obedience to His bidding, so we redeemed humans worship God both vocally and vitally, but it is the worship of a life submitted to God's law and will that makes the worship of our lips and emotions acceptable before the Throne of God.

Christ is worthy to be worshipped by both our lips and our lives, but most of us have difficulty developing our speaking ability. Learning how to communicate with God in a worshipful manner is a learnable art that has many examples demonstrated in the Bible. We call it *prayer.*

Now when He had taken the scroll, the four living creatures and the twenty-four elders fell down before the Lamb, each having a harp, and golden bowls full of incense, *which are the prayers of the saints.*
—Revelation 5:8 (emphasis added)

— 5 —

Worship Involves Prayer

It is probable that the word *prayer* invokes more guilt among Protestants than does the word *sin*, for, although Bible-believing Christians feel a responsibility to pray, few have developed the discipline of prayer. For many, prayer is a desperate cry for help in emergencies, not too unlike a phone call to AAA after the car runs out of gas on the freeway. For others, prayer becomes an abortive attempt to manipulate God. Through formulas, fastings, promises, and praises, they seek to enlist God to do their bidding.

With such primitive concepts of prayer, it is little wonder, then, that prayer is praised publicly but is passed over privately. When prayer is reduced to management of God, it is obviously far too great a chore for the common person. If, however, prayer could become a channel of communication between man and God, what a delightful privilege it would become. Prayer could be an exchange between friends, a communication of guidance, or the channel for love to flow between the redeemed and the Redeemer.

WORSHIP IN HEAVEN
INCLUDES PRAYER

Since even the disciples, who lived, walked, and worked with Jesus during His days on the earth, had to ask Him to " 'teach us to pray, as John also taught his disciples' " (Luke 11:1), it should come as no great surprise that we don't instinctively know how to pray. All communication is a learnable art, and prayer is no exception.

When Moses was instructed to build the Tabernacle in the Wilderness, he was shown a pattern of it while he was on Mount Sinai with God. God clearly said, " 'See that you make all things according to the pattern shown you on the mountain' " (Hebrews 8:5). The imperative for Moses to follow explicitly the pattern given to him was to insure that the scale model on earth was consistent with the heavens themselves.

This is as true of worship, and of the elements that make up worship, as it was of the Tabernacle. We lack totally pure worship here on this earth, so we must look into the heavens to find the pure pattern. The same is true of prayer, for much of our praying here on earth is selfish, need-oriented, and lacking in faith. Jesus brought heaven's prayer to earth, and John brought us into heaven to see prayer there. It is only as we observe heaven's prayer that we have a pattern worth copying. If we will follow the pattern, we will have a miniature heaven on earth. This is in harmony with the Lord's Prayer, which says, " 'Your kingdom come. Your will be done On earth as it is in heaven' " (Matthew 6:10).

FORMS OF HEAVENLY PRAYER

Prayer in heaven, as on the earth, is a channel of communication, and in the book of Revelation we see at least three forms of prayer being used by heaven's residents. For instance, we see the most common form of prayer, *petition*, being used by the waiting martyrs as "they cried with a loud voice, saying, 'How long, O Lord, holy and true, until You judge and avenge our blood on those who dwell on the earth?' " (Revelation 6:10). This is petition. They were asking God how much longer they would have to wait before seeing Divine justice meted out on their persecutors.

The second form of prayer that is obvious in heaven is *communication*. The prayer song of the saints who had gained victory over the beast asked for nothing; it was merely a joyful communication with God (*see* Revelation 15:2-4).

A third form of prayer is *communion*. The living creatures and the twenty-four elders, in the midst of a worship experience, cried out, " 'You are worthy, O Lord, To receive glory and honor and power; For You created all things, And by Your will they exist and were created' " (Revelation 4:11). This has no petition in it at all, and it certainly goes beyond the borders of mere communication. They were seeking to express deep inner feelings about God as an act of communion. It is not too unlike two lovers seeking to share their deep feelings for each other through the use of words. The words are far less important than the feelings they seek to convey through those words.

One thing becomes obvious by observing prayer in heaven: prayer is more than a desire or thought—it is

77

the expression of that desire and that thought. Until thoughts are expressed, they have not reached the prayer level; they are merely meditation, cogitation, or worry. Thoughts must be formed into words and focused on Jesus to become prayer. When you hear someone say, "I have been praying about this matter day and night for weeks," you can be well assured that they have been thinking about it or worrying over it, but it is highly unlikely that they have been spending that much time in actual prayer. Prayer is more than mental gymnastics; it is petition to God, communication unto God, or communion with God.

PRAYER AS INCENSE

Twice in the book of Revelation, prayer is pictured as incense. This imagery comes from the Old Testament Tabernacle in the Wilderness, where incense was burned continually before the Lord upon the Golden Altar. This altar was situated in the Holy Place directly in front of the veil that separated the Holy Place from the Holy of Holies. Coals of fire from the Brazen Altar in the Outer Court were placed on the Golden Altar daily, and every time a priest entered the Holy Place, whether to trim the wicks on the Lamp-stand, add oil to the lamps, set the Table of Shewbread, or worship the Lord, he was commanded to take a handful of incense and sprinkle it upon these glowing coals. This produced a cloud of smoke that went through the veil into the Presence of God, for this was the one action of the priesthood that was performed exclusively unto God. The New Testament calls this smoke "the prayers of the saints" (Revelation 5:8).

It is prayer, praise, and adoration, which, of course, are worship.

The fragrance was compounded according to a formula given to Moses by God in the mount. Four principal spices were blended together, signifying that neither prayer nor worship is a simple action—both are complex, and their components are blended according to a Divine prescription. Furthermore, God prohibited the use of this fragrance anywhere else in the camp of Israel. This prohibition carried a death penalty, for God did not want worship to be faked. The priest who had offered incense came out from the Presence of God smelling just like the Holy Place. It was a testimony to all who came to offer sacrifices that this priest had worshipped the Almighty God. For an Israelite to compound such a fragrance for his personal use would cause others to think that he, too, had been in God's Presence. Religion is given to pretense, but Jesus taught us that " 'God is Spirit, and those who worship Him must worship in spirit and truth' " (John 4:24).

Perhaps this prohibition also signified that making worship a mere pleasure to the natural man—whether sensuous, as music, or as eloquence to delight the natural mind—is always condemned by God. If our motivation for worshipiing God is to have scintillating sensations speeding up and down our spines, we are in a dangerous position with God. There may well be sensations, but they are reactions, not the motivation for the actions.

It is easy, in striving for excellence, to have a quality choir, orchestrated music, and beautifully choreographed dancers whose performances are culturally superb but lacking the touch of God. Any attempt at a worship experience that does not have its roots in prayer is doomed to smell more of earthly flesh than of heavenly fragrance. Those who have never experienced being in the Presence of God may feel that the fragrance is great, but those who have found their way into the Holy Place will know that it is not the fragrance of God but is the fragrance of a worldly substitute for God. The Church desperately needs to know that anything done in any service expressly to give the people a sensual or intellectual thrill is a substitute for the presence of God. Worship begins in prayer, and it must flow Godward through the prayer channel. Where there is no prayer, there will be no worship! Because this is true, prayerlessness is the greatest enemy to worship in the churches of America.

WORSHIP OCCURS AT THE GOLDEN ALTAR

Worship, both in the Tabernacle and in heaven, was offered at the Golden Altar, for this is the *only* altar in heaven. The Brazen Altar, which pictures the cross, has done its work here on the earth. "We have been sanctified through the offering of the body of Jesus Christ once for all" (Hebrews 10:10). So complete was the vicarious death of Christ Jesus that the entire sacrificial system was put away. The issue of sin has been settled forever, so the work of the cross needs no heavenly continuation. Blood deals with sin, guilt, and condemnation, none of which is involved in worship, for the blood must have done its work before we are allowed to enter into the Holy Place. The Old Testament priest stopped by the Laver en route from the Brazen Altar to the Golden Altar, and there he washed every residue of blood and filth from his hands and feet. When he approached the Golden Altar, his hands smelled of incense, not of blood.

It is not at the cross that worship is offered, but before the Throne. The Golden Altar was as close to the throne as the priests could come, with the exception of the high priest, who annually stepped through the veil to stand directly before the Mercy Seat, which was God's throne on earth. But in heaven the worshippers are pictured as standing directly before the Throne of Almighty God, with no separating veil.

God's Word does not make provision for returning to the cross for worship, but it does make provision for progression to the Golden Altar, where, before the Throne, we offer worship unto the Lord God Almighty. We bow at the Golden Altar that stands between us and God—between the Holy Place and the Holy of Holies. Since Christ has made us "priests to His God and Father" (Revelation 1:6), like Zacharias, the father of John the Baptist, whose "lot fell to burn incense when he went into the temple of the Lord" (Luke 1:9), we are invited into the holy presence of God to burn the incense of prayer and worship.

It is incense—not blood—that carries our worship before the Father, and since worship is a never-ending relationship between God and man, the Golden Altar is eternal. It is our prayers, praises, supplications, and adorations that waft our worship from earth into heaven, and these expressions of our inner being will be released to God eternally. Prayer is not merely an earthly function; it is an eternal ministry. We will never mature spiritually beyond the worship of God, and prayer is the channel by which our worship is brought into God's presence.

PRAYER IS INTEGRAL
TO WORSHIP ON EARTH

In Christ's final teaching session with His disciples just prior to His arrest and subsequent crucifixion, He talked of being the True Vine and of the necessity of our abiding as branches in the vine. In the midst of this illustration, Jesus said, " 'If you abide in Me, and My words abide in you, you will ask what you desire, and it shall be done for you' " (John 15:7).

The most common interpretation of this passage is that Christ was establishing the law of harvest, wherein the source of life that produces a spiritual harvest must flow from Christ, the Vine, but the fruit will be produced and displayed on the branches—the disciples. This is sound exegesis that has proved to be as practical in reality as it is profound in religious concept. What is often overlooked, however, is that Jesus stated that *prayer* is the means of maintaining that vital abiding relationship and is also the channel through which the life of the vine is transmitted to the lowly branch. Prayer is the "sap" of the vineyard. When it flows, life will manifest itself, but when it ceases to flow, the leaves turn brown and fall off, the fruit withers on the vine, and the plant goes into its dormant stage. Prayer is therefore not elective but essential: no prayer—no life flow; no life flow—no fruit.

"ABIDE IN ME" = *RELATIONSHIP*

Christ's formula for a sustained life flow can be called "the three "As" of prayer (AAA). The first *A* is *abiding in Christ*, for if we have no relationship, we have no basis for prayer.

Dr. Luke, the writing physician, recorded that "it came to pass, as He [Jesus] was praying in a certain place, when He ceased, that one of His disciples said to Him, 'Lord, teach us to pray, as John also taught his disciples.' So He said to them, 'When you pray, say: Our Father in heaven, Hallowed be Your name' " (Luke 11:1, 2a).

Students of the Greek language say that Christ used an endearing term such as "dear daddy," or "father dear," or "papa." The disciples were not taught to address "the Lord God Almighty" or "the Creator of the universe," for Jesus was seeking to emphasize that the foundation for all of our praying is the warmth and intimacy of our relationship with God. True prayer will always have its roots in a proper relationship with God, for in prayer we are neither managing nor manipulating God; we are relating to Him.

If prayer is viewed as a submission of petitions to Almighty God, we will pray only out of and in the midst of our needs, but prayer should not begin when problems arise; the Scriptures teach that prayer starts with relationships that *precede* problems. One of the poorest times to learn to pray is when the pilot has just announced that the last engine on the jet has quit.

There are at least eight levels of prayer taught in the Scriptures, and petition is the second level. But even this level demands relationship, for petitioning prayer is communication between two parties, one needy and the other capable of supplying that need. Just because another can supply your need does not mean that he has a responsibility or desire to meet your need. There are persons living in my area who could totally meet my financial needs, but I have no relationship with them. They have no knowledge of me, and the chances of their ever underwriting me and my ministry are so remote that my calculator can't even figure the possibility factor. Similarly, just because God is able to do "exceedingly abundantly above all that we ask or think" (Ephesians 3:20) does not mean that He is honor-bound to respond to our every wish. God responds to relationship, not needs, and the relationship that He has offered us is an ongoing relationship requiring communication. The Scriptures challenge us to have a life of prayer, not a word of prayer, for we cannot maintain a maturing relationship without ongoing communication.

For several years I have traveled widely throughout the world to share my ministry. Much of the time my wife remains at home. To prevent this separation from damaging our marriage, I phone home at least daily, and occasionally twice a day, just to keep the lines of communication open. There obviously is not enough business to necessitate such frequent calls, but there is a need for us to relate on the daily matters of life to such a full extent that our relationship together is constantly kept current. In order for us to keep a close communion, we must keep a constant communication, and what we talk about is far less important than the fact that we talk.

Isn't this same principle valid in our relationship with God? What we talk about in prayer is far less important than the fact that we are spending time talking with God. God is as interested in hearing about the things that are important to me as I am in hearing my wife talk about the things that are important to her. We need not talk "spiritual" talk to God, nor do we need to use

King James English. God talked "man talk" with Adam
and Noah, and Gabriel talked "woman talk" to Mary. The
communication of prayer is far more important than
what is communicated, for the very act of prayer
strengthens and enlarges our relationship with God.

Perhaps our greatest hindrance to prayer is the
concept that we must talk "God talk," wherein we show
our ignorance by talking His subject. When our
relationship with God becomes sufficiently mature that
we are comfortable in talking to Him about the things we
know, we will be amazed to discover how knowledgeable
God is in our field. I have found that God knows a great
deal about architecture and construction as well as child-
raising and relating to people. My wife has often been
aided by God in her cooking and household duties. I never
cease to be amazed at how smart God is!

We need to remind ourselves that the true purpose
of prayer is not to get God to see things as we see
them, but to be able to see things as God sees them.
God's perspective is so different from ours. He views
events as they affect the entire Body of Christ, not merely
as they affect an individual member in that Body. Paul's
perspective of being imprisoned in a crude Roman jail
was vastly inferior to God's view until he talked it over
with God; then he could write, "I want you to know,
brethren, that the things which have happened to me
have actually turned out for the furtherance of the
gospel, so that it has become evident to the whole palace
guard, and to all the rest, that my chains are in Christ"
(Philippians 1:12, 13).

The relationship with God that prayer offers lets us
see from the top instead of from the bottom of the heap.

Often prayer does not change circumstances at all, but it marvelously changes our attitude toward those circumstances.

"MY WORDS ABIDE IN YOU" = *FELLOWSHIP*

As an element of worship, prayer is the medium that maintains a relationship with God that is fundamental to worship. But this same prayer channel can bring us into a fellowship with God that causes the Bible to become a speaking Book to us. True prayer must be a two-way communication, not a monologue. God's communication to us is as vital as, if not more vital than, our prayer to Him, for prayer is not merely finding a quiet place where we can give God "unknown information"; it is finding a quiet time when you and God can talk.

How often we make our way to a quiet place of prayer, express our petitions to God, and then rush back to the activities of life without even waiting for a reply. Either we didn't believe that God heard us, or we lacked faith to believe that He would answer us. I long ago learned that when placing a phone call, I should not start speaking while the phone is still ringing, for until the called party answers, there can be no communication no matter how loudly or eloquently I may speak. Perhaps we could let meditation and praise place the call to heaven, and then when we know God is "on the line," we can begin to communicate with Him.

In Christ's illustration, our abiding in Christ is a union or a joining of the branch to the vine. Christ's words *abiding in us* are a flow of life from the roots to the leaves and fruit. Abiding in Christ, is, indeed, *relationship*, but having Christ's words abiding in us produces an intimate

86

fellowship—the life of God flowing into the praying person.

All of us have experienced relationships that did not have genuine fellowship in them. I have stood awkwardly as I was introduced to relatives of mine, for although we were indeed related, we did not know one another, and we had nothing in common to talk about except our family name. Similarly, some Christians are rightly related to the Lord Jesus Christ, and yet they have not developed an intimate fellowship that makes talking together a pleasurable experience.

Throughout the Bible, God has chosen to reveal Himself to mankind through the introduction of His name. It has been a progressive manifestation wherein each addition to His name unfolded a different facet of His Divine nature. The compound names of God given to us in the Old Testament unfold God in rich, revealing tones. These names of God picture His nature, and Jesus told us that our approach to God was to be "in My name" (*see* John 14: 13, 14). Still, the psalmist declared, "You have magnified Your word above all Your name" (Psalm 138:2). God has pledged to honor what He has said even above what He is. This is, of course, for our sakes, for we have a written record of what He has said, but we do not have a photograph of what He is. God confidently assures us that if He said it, that settles it! He will honor that promise more highly than He honors the revelation of Himself through His names.

Whether or not we are comfortable with it, God is not honor-bound to meet needs, but He has promised to honor what He has said. If the basis of our prayers is need, we must plead mercy, but if the basis of our prayers is the promises of God, then we can pray according to God's Word, and God has committed Himself to answer His Word.

In my last pastorate, we had prayer services every morning of the week. Prayer requests could be placed in the offering plates, or they could be phoned in to our "hotline" day or night. These requests were presented before the Lord each morning, and they were recorded in a "book of remembrance" with a space left blank for writing in the date when we were informed that the prayer had been answered.

One day the Lord made me aware that the people coming to the prayer services arrived strong and enthusiastic but left the services haggard and worn out. He also informed me that it was my fault! "You have taught the people to get involved with the problems and not the promises," He said.

I realized how wrong I had been. We had been wrestling with the problems of other people for months. We had informed God of the great needs, instructed Him in what He should do to meet those needs, and implied that He should report back to us when He was finished.

For a season I personally conducted the prayer meetings to retrain my congregation. I would read a series of requests for a particular need, and then I would ask the prayer partners for some promises of God that applied to this need. When we had quoted several, I had the people stand and praise God for His promises; then I asked them, "How many of you feel that those promises meet these needs?" After a show of hands, I invited them to join me in praising God that His provision did, indeed, meet these problems.

It was a new form of praying for all of us, but the results were amazing. We had far more reports of answered prayer that week than we had received in previous weeks, and as a glorious byproduct, we found ourselves leaving the prayer meetings refreshed, strengthened, and encouraged rather than exhausted and emotionally spent. Pleading the promises is a positive form of praying that produces powerful results, for it allows God's Word to flow through us.

Actually, prayer is really not so much petition as it is proclamation. We are proclaiming the Word of God. When we proclaim God's Word rather than declare our "wants," we find ourselves pleading God's will, which releases God to meet our needs and fulfill our wants. Focusing our prayer time and energy on our abiding relationship with God, and learning to rejoice in the promises of His Word, help us break through to a higher dimension in prayer.

Oswald Chambers wrote, "The meaning of prayer is that we get hold of God, not the answer." In my religious heritage we had a common expression: "I've prayed through." By this we meant that we had continued to pray concerning a situation until we were convinced that we had touched God. This awareness gave both an inner peace and an assurance that what we had asked would be granted in God's own good time and way. We had touched God—we had prayed through.

It is sad that more people are through praying than ever pray through. Perhaps prayer has been set aside because we have failed to realize the depth of fellowship with God that it offers. We may have lost the realization that there is more than the legal relationship that has placed us in Christ Jesus; there is the discipline of worship that causes God's very Word to flow in us. That fellowship can become so rich and intimate as to bring about a partnership relationship with God.

"ASK" = *PARTNERSHIP*

The third *A* in Jesus' formula for prayer is " '*Ask* what you desire, and it shall be done for you' " (John 15:7, italics mine). I have been told that the construction of the Greek wording here allows the literal translation "If it is not around, We'll make it for you." God so desires to meet your request that if you can want something that He has not already created, He will make it for you on the spot. Paul had such assurance, for he wrote, "My God shall supply all your need according to His riches in glory by Christ Jesus" (Philippians 4:19). God has pledged the supply; He has backed that pledge with all the riches in heaven; and He has chosen Christ Jesus to be the channel through which that supply will be delivered.

Recently my attention was again drawn to this verse in Philippians which speaks of Paul's confidence in God's ability and willingness to supply from His resources. William Barclay has translated this verse as "My God will supply everything you need out of the splendour of His wealth given you in Christ Jesus." In checking the word "need," I found that both Young and Strong call it "necessity," while Thayer translates it as "things which you can scarcely be without." My mind at once thought of it this way: "God will give all needed supplies."

I could immediately apply this in my office situation. I am blessed with a highly qualified secretary, without whom my traveling ministry would be greatly restricted.

By keeping in contact with her by phone, I am able to be on the road more than three weeks of every month. She maintains the office, keeps the correspondence current, and looks after the schedule. On the few days per month that I am in the office, it would be devastating to me to have Cheryl come in, get on her knees, look up at me, and say, "Oh, Dr. Cornwall, generous man of God, could you find it in your heart to finance the purchase of some typewriter ribbons and paper? We are out of supplies, and I cannot do any more work without them." Because of the working partnership that we have established, I cannot afford to let her be without needed supplies, so I have an open account at an office supply outlet. Cheryl need not ask me for supplies; I have authorized her to order anything that is needed to turn out the work.

In pledging to provide for us all needed supplies, God is acknowledging a partnership relationship with us. Paul declared, "We are God's fellow workers" (1 Corinthians 3:9), and "We . . . [are] workers together with Him" (2 Corinthians 6:1). Prayer, then, is not manipulation of God; it is communication with God on a partnership level.

The longer I live, the greater is my conviction that strong relationships negate the need for strong petitions. Let us illustrate this principle with contrasting stories.

When I visit major cities in India or Indonesia, I can expect to encounter some of the most proficient beggars in the world. Being white, and American, I am automatically viewed as wealthy, so I become a target for their supplications. They look pathetic, and if they can speak English they will tell a story designed to evoke extreme pity in me. If what I see and hear does not cause me to give as much as they think I should have shared, they will get on their knees, bow their foreheads onto my shoetops, and begin a most woeful wailing. If *this* doesn't induce me to give sufficiently, they will hold onto my coattail or crawl on their knees behind me, crying something equivalent to "Cheapskate! Cheapskate!" At times it becomes necessary for me to secure the help of the doorman at the hotel to get rid of them.

Why do they work so hard on me? They know that they will never see me again; that since they have no relationship with me whatsoever, if they hope to get anything from me they had better get it while I am there. This is the way many Christians pray. Lacking on ongoing relationship with God, they become desperate in their pleadings on the rare occasions that they find themselves in God's presence.

In contrast to this is an incident that took place during the spring of 1984. On Mother's Day of that year we were to have all three of our daughters home for the first time in eighteen years. My missionary daughter returned home in 1983, and my daughter who is married to an Argentine architect was flying home with her entire family to live in the United States. Our oldest daughter had flown in from college, where she is upgrading her degree in nursing, to make the family reunion complete. My wife and I had planned this for more than a year.

Unfortunately for me, Mother's Day falls on a Sunday, and I am very rarely home on Sundays. Saturday afternoon I had just finished packing my suitcase when my wife, Eleanor, came into the bedroom and said, "Honey, I'm so excited about tomorrow that I forgot to go to the bank to get some money. Our plans call for me to take everyone to the restaurant for dinner, but I'm broke. I know that you carry a hundred-dollar bill for emergencies. This is an emergency; may I have it?"

She didn't get down on her knees and beg; she didn't even promise me a special dinner when I returned. She merely said, "You have it; I need it; please give it to me." Her petition was based on a forty-one-year relationship that has convinced her that anything she needs, I will supply if it is within the realm of my ability.

Isn't this what prayer is all about? Our relationship with God gives us the authority to "come boldly to the throne of grace, that we may obtain mercy and find grace to help in time of need" (Hebrews 4:16). Unquestionably, the most effective prayer is based on God's Word and flows out of an intimate relationship with Christ Jesus.

Prayer is as integral to worship on earth as it is in heaven, and the three basic forms of prayer that we have viewed in heaven are part of the worship here on earth if earthly prayer follows the heavenly pattern. Most praying Christians have an awareness that prayer can be prayed as petition, communication, or communion, but not all of them understand what each form of prayer does, so they often use the wrong type of prayer in their approach to God.

PRAYER AS *PETITION*

Prayer as petition *releases God to action*. This form of prayer would also include supplication and inter-cession, for they are, of course, merely strong forms of petition, usually on behalf of another. The need to ask God for anything has bothered many Christians, for they

93

say, "If God is our gracious heavenly Father, why doesn't He automatically do for us what needs to be done?"

Such questioning demonstrates a lack of understanding of the authority God has restored to the Church on earth. The breaking of the seals on the scroll evidenced Christ's intervention in the role of Kinsman-Redeemer. He redeemed us back to God and the earth back to us. The dominion given to Adam, and lost in the fall of man, is now vested in Christ's Church. Far more than we realize, we are in charge down here.

God, Who is absolute authority, understands the workings of a chain of command, and He never violates it, for a chain of command is useless unless it is followed. God does not even violate what rights Satan has in this hour, so He certainly will not violate the rights and authority He has given to His Church, especially since it cost Him such a price to restore that authority to us. God won't even go over the head of a local pastor. The membership may, but God will not.

Since it is clearly declared that believers have been made "kings and priests unto God" (*see* Revelation 1:6, 5:10), the relational authority we have as co-regents with Christ Jesus is high on this chain of command, and God dares not intervene in any thing on this earth over which the Church has accepted command. Regardless of how badly we perform in executing our authorities here, God will not intervene unless we ask for help. This creates the problem that as long as we feel able to do the task, we will have no outside assistance, for we have as much liberty to fail as to succeed.

We are not, however, limited to our own resources in the administering of our earthly authority. All of the wisdom, power, authority, and personnel of heaven are available to us for the asking. Like the traffic patrolman who has the backing of the state militia and the federal troops, if needed, so our backup resources are limitless for the asking.

Perhaps we can gain understanding by looking at a hypothetical life situation. Let's assume that you purchase a home that lacks a fence, but since you have small children and a dog, a fenced-in yard is important to you. Your neighbor, however, informs you that he is opposed to having a fence between his property and yours, for it has been unfenced for years and he likes it that way. Upon checking at the city hall, you find that there are no legal restrictions against having a fence, so you apply for and receive a permit to construct a fence.

Although you follow the building code accurately, your neighbor protests, and eventually "takes the law into his own hands" by tearing down the fence. Immediately you phone the police, and after the investigating officer examines your permit and the remains of the fence, he tells you that your legal rights have been violated. He even volunteers the information that they have had difficulties with this neighbor in the past and that he personally is delighted to have an opportunity to "throw the book" at the troublesome neighbor. Then the officer asks you to come down to the police station to sign a complaint against the neighbor.

Protesting that signing a complaint is unnecessary and that all you want is to have the neighbor arrested will likely gain you the information that since the officer did not witness the crime, he cannot arrest the fence-destroyer without a warrant. Your signed complaint will authorize him to intervene on your behalf, but no complaint—no arrest.

Similarly, prayer signs a complaint against the opposition. Prayer says, "God, that neighbor knocked down my fence. Will You get him for me?"

God responds, "I've been waiting for this chance for months. Sign a complaint with petitioning prayer, and I'll gladly intervene on your behalf."

James 4:2 is so elementary that few Christians believe it: "You do not have because you do not ask." We wish for, yearn after, and weep over, but until we actually ask for it, we have not prayed a prayer of petition.

PRAYER AS *COMMUNICATION*

Communicative prayer informs God of our attitudes as well as of our desires. It includes thanksgiving and praise, for these are very positive expressions of communication to God. While petition tells God of our needs, communication *informs God of our nature*. It reveals whether we are positive or negative, praying in faith or in fear. It demonstrates whether we are selfish or selfless in our petitions, and it shows whether we are dealing with the problem or with the Person of Christ. Actually, if we will just pay attention to what we are saying when we are communicating with God, we will learn a great deal about our own nature—discovering whether we are moving in the flesh or in the Spirit.

Beyond unfolding our nature, communicative prayer *reveals our concepts of God*. More can be learned of a person's concept of the Divine by listening to his prayers than by hearing his sermons or testimony. I remember a minister whom I called to my church two or more times a year for several consecutive years. I instructed the sound-room personnel to record all of his public prayers. I am not certain that I ever listened to a playback of one of his sermons, but I listened to those prayers again and again. That man knew God, and when he prayed, he revealed his concepts of God in ways he seemed unable to do in his sermons. My understanding of God was greatly enlarged by listening to that man pray.

Communicating with God—praying—reveals whether we view God as austere or approachable, as judgmental or loving. The very way we approach God in prayer reveals our deep inner concepts of Him. The tone of voice that is employed, the vocabulary used, and even the body language or lack of it, all unveil some of our concepts of God.

Prayer that is not particularly asking God for something, but rather is merely a time of talking with God as a Person we love, also *unveils our inner attitudes toward God.* It demonstrates to God, to ourselves, and to anyone listening whether we are submitted to God's will or are seeking to manipulate God to our will. It rather rapidly reveals whether we are walking in obedience to God or in obstinacy. Perhaps the reason that some persons who desire to worship will not pray is because they do not want to face the self-revelation that is produced by talking with God; but the first step to change is an awareness of a need to change, and communication with God will produce an instant checklist.

97

Communicating openly with God will also *show whose glory is foremost* in our thoughts. Are we concerned with His worthiness or with ours? Are we asking to be vindicated, or is God's glory uppermost in our thoughts? Would the answer to our prayer benefit us or God the most? These questions are generally answered in the course of our talking with God.

Long ago we learned that if you don't want people to know the "real" you—the inner you—don't talk. If you do not want to know your inner self, don't pray, for the prayer of communication is like a full-length mirror to your soul. Jesus declared, " 'Out of the abundance of the heart the mouth speaks' " (Matthew 12:34), or, as I have often quoted my version from the pulpit, "Out of the abundance of the heart the mouth blabs!" My soul tends to run out of my mouth when the floodgate of my tongue is released. This is a real imperative for worship, for until our inner attitudes are expressed honestly to God, we have not worshipped.

PRAYER AS *COMMUNION*

When we looked at heaven's pattern for prayer, we saw redeemed persons communicating with God through the prayer channel. Prayer as communion includes submission and adoration, and it *fellowships with God in all of His actions*. It induces a blending of our spirit with God's Spirit. It so submits to God that there is an automatic volunteering to do His will, much like Isaiah, after being purged by the coal from the heavenly altar, when he heard himself saying, " 'Here am I! Send me' " (Isaiah 6:8). There is an amazing blending of spirit with Spirit in communion prayer. It is probably the highest form of prayer that a person can pray, and it leads to the highest level of worship into which any of us can enter. This prayer may contain less speaking than the other two forms of prayer, but it will have life-changing results, for it is two persons becoming so intertwined as to function as one. Communion prayer is as close to walking with God in the garden of Eden as we will experience while still residents of this earth.

To sum this up: The **premise** of prayer is *relationship, fellowship,* and *partnership.* The **pattern** of our prayer is *petition, communication,* and *communion,* while the **purpose** of prayer is *change*—change in us, in circumstances, and in our union with God. The praying person will not remain the same; he will either change or cease to truly pray. (Mere religious recitations do not count as prayer.)

Prayer cannot successfully be separated from worship, for it prepares the soul for worship, expresses the spirit in worship, and interacts with God, which is worship.

Worship without prayer is like daytime without light, a school without students, a choir without music, or an automobile without fuel.

Prayer is the *entrance* to our worship, the *energy* of our worship, the *expression* of our worship, and the *enhancer* of our worship.

Prayer *establishes* worship, *embraces* worship, *enlarges* worship, and *enlightens* our worship.

The praying saint cannot keep from worshipping; the prayerless saint cannot rise to worship.

In heaven, prayer is typified as incense, and that incense is offered before the Presence of God as a sweet-smelling savor that is most pleasing to God. It is so pleasing, in fact, that God has the prayers recorded so that they may be played back repeatedly.

When we couple the action recorded in Revelation 8:3 with this incense that is mentioned in Revelation 5, we discover that prayer is blended—heaven's and earth's prayers are intermingled before they come to the Throne of God.

Then another angel, having a golden censer, came and stood at the altar. And he was given much incense, that he should offer it with the prayers of all the saints upon the golden altar which was before the throne.
—Revelation 8:3

— 6 —

Worship Manifests a Blending

Since the pattern and formula for everything that was connected with the Old Testament Tabernacle in the Wilderness was given to Moses by God, we are correct in looking for a spiritual application for the entire Tabernacle. The incense, which typified prayer and worship, was compounded of four principal spices, which had been broken from the bush, beaten into a powder, blended together, and then burned as a compound. Among the lessons this teaches is the obvious truth that worship is a blending of a variety of ingredients. Just as frankincense alone would not suffice as an incense to be burned before God, so no one element in the worship process may stand alone and be acceptable before God.

WORSHIP NEEDS HOMOGENIZATION
In our everyday life we have come to accept the convenience of homogenization. This process, which breaks up the fat globules and other solids of milk or cream by means of a homogenizer to attain a uniform state of consistency through reduction to blending,

guarantees us a consistent blend of milk and cream down to the last glass of milk in the container. We now use this same process to give us smooth, even peanut butter, as well as paint that does not need continual stirring. Baby food and cosmetics have long been homogenized by reducing the particles to uniform size and distributing them evenly throughout the product. It is likely that true worship needs similar treatment.

Every cook knows that a cake is not merely flour, milk, eggs, butter, sugar, and flavoring placed in a pan and then baked. The cake may comprise these ingredients, but the blending of these ingredients greatly affects the texture and flavor of that cake. Similarly, worship is more than the correct ingredients brought together in one place. Worship requires such a harmonizing of the separate parts that they become evenly distributed throughout the whole worship process, even to the point of losing their individual characteristics. Just as lumpy gravy indicates poor blending and mixing, so "lumpy" worship evidences an unblended mixing of components.

WORSHIP INVOLVES A BLENDING OF HEAVEN AND EARTH

John's view of worship in heaven showed him that the four living creatures and the twenty-four elders did not come before God in worship empty-handed; they came "each having a harp, and golden bowls full of incense, which are the prayers of the saints" (Revelation 5:8). In one hand they brought music, and in the other hand they had a bowl full of the prayers of the saints on earth. These bowls, or vials, are Divine containers of our prayers.

104

Perhaps they could be called storage jars, love letters, or recordings. If John were writing this letter today, he might call them floppy disks, for when a computer operator has assembled the desired information or program on the screen, he records it on a floppy disk for backup and permanent storage. This information can be recalled at will, very much as a record can be played repeatedly on a phonograph.

So valuable is prayer that it is not only recorded but is put into the hands of these heavenly representatives for both safe-keeping and constant review. Prayer that touches God is not lost once it is prayed, for all prayer that reaches heaven is kept as a sweet, fragrant incense to be offered to God again and again.

Prayer is also seen as incense a little later in this book, for we read, "Then another angel, having a golden censer, came and stood at the altar. And he was given much incense, that he should offer it with the prayers of all the saints upon the golden altar which was before the throne" (Revelation 8:3). Not only has heaven appointed twenty-eight of its highest inhabitants to keep track of the prayers that ascend from the earth, but God has also appointed a special angel whose task is to mix the incense of heaven with the incense of earth so that it will have the proper fragrance when it comes before the Throne of God.

We earth-bound creatures usually do not know how to pray perfect prayers. Our prayers are often selfish and limited to our perspective. Our incense often smells "fleshly," but the prayers of the saints who have been perfected in the presence of God are correct in every respect. Unhindered by fleshly desires and appetites, and unrestrained in their view of the will and plan of God, these saints faithfully pray according to the will of God, and their heavenly prayers are blended by this mighty angel with the earthly prayers held in storage by the living creatures and the elders.

The writer of the book of Hebrews declared, "But you have come to Mount Zion and to the city of the living God, the heavenly Jerusalem, to an innumerable company of angels, to the general assembly and church of the firstborn who are registered in heaven, to God the Judge of all, to the spirits of just men made perfect, to Jesus the Mediator of the new covenant, and to the blood of sprinkling that speaks better things than that of Abel" (Hebrews 12:22-24). This is not written in the future tense, as something to which we look forward, but clearly states that we *"have* come"—signifying that there is a time, a moment, a season, when the saints on earth join the saints in heaven, for we are one family that has been geographically divided.

When does this family get together? During worship. When the prayer channel from earth is releasing worship heavenward, heaven gets involved so that the worship will be pure, perfect, and presentable before the Throne of God. The angel with the golden censer blends heaven's incense with earth's incense, homogenizing them into a perfect blend. Earth's petition and praise are mingled with heaven's worship and adoration to create the perfect worship experience.

Some persons, although feeling motivated to pray, neglect entering into prayer for lack of a prayer partner, but this passage would seem to indicate that while we may not have a partner here on earth, individual prayer is next to impossible, for the prayer immediately becomes the concern of the living creatures, the elders, and the angels. Heaven's prayer partners are always on standby alert just waiting for a prayer to ascend from the earth. Perhaps, in a manner not yet revealed to us, our prayers are blended with the prayers of Abel, Moses, Joshua, David, Jesus, Martin Luther, Charles Spurgeon, and thousands times thousands times ten thousands of our spiritual brothers and sisters who would love to tell us, "If you'll start it, I'll join it." Our prayers are accelerated by their prayers, our praise is amplified by their praise, and our worship is purified by the worship of these residents of heaven. Whatever we may lack in faith, motivation, consecration, or earnestness, they are more than able to compensate on our behalf.

INDIVIDUAL DIFFERENCES
ENHANCE WORSHIP

As vital as the blending of heaven and earth is to worship, it is but one of several blends needed for worship to be at its highest level. This fifth chapter of Revelation unveils a melting together in worship of the living creatures (verse 6), the elders (verse 8), the angels (verse 11), "and every creature which is in heaven and on the earth and under the earth and such as are in the sea, and all that are in them . . ." (Revelation 5:13). Worship in heaven includes all of its inhabitants, and the very act of worship seems to homogenize them into one functioning unit.

Here on earth, the saints, though seemingly loving to sing "We are not divided," are divided nonetheless by religious heritage, doctrine, practice, and even socio-economic strata. Each group may develop its own set of rituals, but worship of separate groups is almost like burning one spice as the worship incense. The best worship is produced when various religious heritages blend in the one activity that transcends doctrine and practice: the worship of God.

In 1977, when the Charismatic movement was at its zenith, the largest convention ever held under the Charismatic banner took place in Kansas City, Missouri. During the day, each denomination represented met in separate facilities, but at night everyone gathered in Arrowhead Stadium—home of the Kansas City Chiefs football team—for a time of praise and worship that will long be remembered by the participants. Massed thousands of people stepped beyond their religious boundaries and worshipped as one united body of believers. You could not tell the Catholics from the Protestants, much less pick out the various branches of Protestantism that were represented in the convention. The very mixture aided the worship, and the blend had a fragrance unlike the worship odor of any one group. Our acceptance of one another as brothers and sisters in Christ helped us to join together in united and spontaneous worship of the common Redeemer. It was not an artificial blending; it was automatic. Christ, not creed, was our concern, and worship, not works, was our activity.

Worship is the one religious activity that lends itself to such a delicate blending of different heritages, for worship is so Christ-centered and requires such a God-consciousness that participants must look away from themselves in order to worship. There will likely remain various areas of disagreement and division in the true

Church until Christ Himself returns to the earth, but there is no reason for us to be divided in the act of worship, for even if our methods of expressing that worship differ, those very differences will lend flavor and color to the worship when homogenized together.

This is true also in the local congregation. Worship is one thing that cannot be done for the people; it must be done by them, for worship by identification is impossible. The Old Testament priesthood assisted the worshipper in his approach to God, but they did not perform the ritual as a surrogate for the worshipper. There was always a close bond between the suppliant and the priest; whatever the ritual, they did it together. It can be no less than this in the New Testament, which declares the priesthood of the believer. The choir's anthem cannot substitute for congregational singing, nor can the preacher's sermon replace congregational praise and worship. Worship demands involvement on the part of the worshipper.

Over the years there has been a steady widening of the gap between the clergy and the laity, and the wider the gap, the greater the exaltation of the professional in the pulpit. From time to time this gap has been bridged, but the cost of maintaining a personal relationship with God has usually been too high for most congregations. They have preferred to declare their pastor as their substitute before God, very much as the children of Israel did at Mount Sinai. Being chosen to act as the people's representative before God, and as God's representative to the people, is heady wine that most clergymen find very difficult to pass, so once again the Church finds Herself reduced to the representative and the represented in the local congregations. The leader, whether he be called pastor, priest, elder, bishop, or simply the preacher, seeks to worship for and in front of his congregation, while the people, who pay his salary, try to identify with what is being done.

It simply cannot work! Worship demands participation. The confession, the repentance, the rejoicing, and the praising must be done by the people themselves. Any prostration, kneeling, standing, or lifting up of hands must be done by everyone who wishes to be involved in the worship experience, just as clapping, dancing, and weeping for joy must be performed by, not for, the people. Worship is not a visual or vicarious experience; it is a "hands-on" experience.

None of this is to be construed as a rejection of Paul's statement that Christ gave pastors to the Church (*see* Ephesians 4:11). We all rejoice in this great gift of leaders of the flock of Christ, but they have been given not as substitutes for the saints but "for the equipping of the saints for the work of ministry" (Ephesians 4:12). The first ministry of any segment of the Body of Christ is ministry unto God. Pastors have been given to the Church to prepare, equip, and lead their congregations into a worship ministry unto God. Teaching another may involve demonstration, but it cannot include substitution.

At least during seasons of worship, it is beneficial if the clergy and the laity can be merged into a "claity." There should be no great ones and no lesser ones, for all are worshippers who have risen to the highest common denominator: worship. Before king David danced before the returning Ark, he removed his kingly garments and girded himself with the simple garb of the priesthood, thereby identifying with them as a worshipper rather than seeking to lead them as their king.

The obvious value of blending a congregation into one unit for worship is that each person in the congregation has different gifts, abilities, talents, and graces from God. God's wisdom, power, and channel of communication are vested in the Holy Spirit, and God has shared His Spirit with individual believers. No one of us has all of God's gifts and graces in his life, but a common sharing of a group of saints makes more of these Divine benefits available to assist us in our worship. Not all of these believers have access to the pulpit, but all have access to God. When the opportunity is given, it is amazing what a parking lot attendant can contribute to a worship experience, or how a homemaker can enhance our awareness of God's Presence in the Church. I have even seen schoolchildren, in their simplistic approach to God, open an entire congregation to a fresh expression of worship to God.

CORPORATE RESPONSE ENLARGES THE WORSHIP EXPERIENCE

No one would deny the beauty of individual worship. David came to know his God through the worship experiences he had while tending his father's sheep as a lonely shepherd, and thousands of persons after him have found their way into the presence of the Divine by worshipping as solitary individuals. This does not, however, detract from the truth that worship generally reaches higher levels of expression when a body of believers is worshipping together.

Some years ago I taught on worship in a convention, and, as my custom is, at the conclusion of the message I asked the people to stand and worship the Lord. To my amazement they went beyond praise and entered into a beautiful realm of worship. I joined them in their worship, and with hands raised and eyes closed was soon caught up in the raptures that only a worshipper experiences.

"Open your eyes and tell Me what you see out there," the Lord spoke to me in my spirit.

Quickly surveying the crowd, I explained to the Lord that some people were kneeling, some were standing, a few were dancing, and some were prostrate before the Lord. Some were singing, others were weeping, and one or two were seated, reading their Bibles.

I had hardly finished describing the scene in front of me when I realized that only in corporate worship can we fully express our inner attitudes toward God. There have been times when the only suitable posture for worship was to completely prostrate myself on the floor before the Lord; but when I did so, I would have an inner awareness that God should be praised with exuberance and joy, but I am not capable of prostration and dancing at the same time. No matter how we choose to express our worship before the Lord, so many other forms of expression remain that we feel frustrated and incomplete in our communication of worship.

It is when we have a group of worshippers together, as in congregational worship, that we are able to more fully express our worship to God, for then all things can be done simultaneously. The variety enhances and enlarges the worship experience.

"Continue to watch what is happening," the Lord said to me.

In the course of just a few minutes I saw a virtual "fruit basket upset." The persons who had been prostrated before the Lord rose and began to dance before His Presence, while those who had been dancing prostrated themselves before Him. Some who had been standing sat down, while others who had been seated reading their Bibles now stood and raised their hands before God's Presence. The scene changed as though I were looking into a kaleidoscope. I viewed it with wonder.

"The lesson I want you to learn," the Lord continued, "is not to make people specialists in the expression of their worship. Allow for variety both corporately and individually. No one action can express all emotions, so allow for multiple actions in each person so that his or her worship can be complete."

Because worship is a complex response of our inner attitudes toward God, it is likely that no one individual can completely and fully express his feelings, but a united group which has not been forced into a conformity of action can express worship in multiple ways. Furthermore, all of us need to avail ourselves of a wide variety of means of expressing our deep love and adoration for the Lord, for a pattern of sameness usually results in staleness. It is all too easy to make a ritual out of something that has been very real to us, and mere ritual seldom retains the power to express deep inner feelings about God.

Corporate worship also offers reinforcement, for the spill-over of the worship of others acts as a primer or goad to our own worship expressions. The sound of other voices praising the Lord and the sight of other persons physically demonstrating their love to Jesus inspire our hearts to renewed vigor in reaching out to God. Many have been the occasions when my own heart has introspectively condemned me and has drawn me away from the Presence of God, but just being in the midst of others who were worshipping shifted my attention away from myself to God Himself, and I entered into worship with them. Little wonder, then, that we are admonished to "consider one another in order to stir up love and good works, not forsaking the assembling of ourselves together, as is the manner of some, but exhorting one another, and so much the more as you see the Day approaching" (Hebrews 10:24, 25).

CULTURAL FACTORS AFFECT WORSHIP

Sameness is not God's goal for worshippers, for He has made us infinitely varied creatures. But some of the differences between races are more cultural than genetic, and quite often the restrictions that culture imposes upon a people limit their ability to worship the Lord. Such cultural characteristics as the Arab restriction upon the public appearance of women, the English trait of showing no outward emotion in public, the German tendency to repress individualism in favor of group action, or the American concept that men don't show tenderness lest they lose their "macho" image, all hinder a full expression of worship.

On my first visit to Holland, the directors of the convention spent much time with me before the first day of the conference, trying to help me understand the Dutch people. I was told of their propensity to commitment and of their courage, and I was also told that they are not an expressive nationality. The leaders advised me that there was no vocal praise in the churches of Holland and that I should not push too hard to bring the people into an action that would violate their very nature.

I did not seek to change the people; I merely showed them in the Word that praise was natural to the children of God, regardless of race, nationality, creed, or inhibition. By the third session the delegates at the conference had broken into a most glorious and exuberant praise. Before the conference was over, every form of expression of praise that I have witnessed in any nation of the earth was being practiced on that conference grounds. God did not make Americans out of the Dutch people, but He did lead them out of some cultural inhibitions that had greatly hindered their responses to Him in praise and worship.

All of us are influenced and inhibited by cultural experiences we have shared in the past. We are taught to conform to our peers, and our capacity to express love is vitally affected by the expression of love we saw in our homes. Quite often these past experiences negatively affect our attempts at worshipping God. For instance, if those close to us could not express love with words and touch, it subconsciously affects our attitudes and approach to God. If our relationship with our brothers and sisters was one of sibling rivalry rather than of camaraderie, our corporate worship experiences will tend to be competitive rather than completive. Apart from the work of God's grace in our lives, we are what we have been taught to be by example and exhortation.

Often times we hide behind cultural inhibitions rather than obey the clear command of the Scriptures to worship the Lord with our intellect, our emotions, and our spirit. I have seen persons lavish far more honest affection and attention on their dog than they do on their God, for they have no cultural barriers to overcome in relating positively to their pet. To insist upon doing only what comes naturally is to limit ourselves to the peer pressure and cultural restraints others have placed upon us, and this means that we will never rise to a level higher than that which others have chosen for us to attain. Christ Jesus came to release us from every bondage and limitation that has kept us from Him, but it will take some conscious cooperation from us to enter into that freedom.

God's goal is not to destroy individuality but to release it. Whenever people are pressed into a mold of conformity, their individuality is stifled, but when they are enabled to respond to God from the honesty of their hearts, the infinite variety that God has keyed into His highest creation manifests itself gloriously. Watching the uninhibited responses of children around the Christmas tree as the presents are being opened will give evidence to the fact that we do not all respond to situations alike. It is disappointing that society will likely erase these differences by the time those children are adults, but God can bring us back to our true nature when we are in His Presence.

Some Christians have been hampered in their worship responses to God by the great inhibitions they observed in their parents. "I'm just like my father," they say. Which father—earthly or spiritual? If the new birth

116

means that we have been born of God, then God is our Father in our new spiritual life, and when responding to Him, we should expect His nature, not the nature of our earthly parentage, to manifest itself. The declared work of the Holy Spirit in this age is to make us to be conformed to the image of God's Son. This means the development of a new nature, and God's nature is very accustomed to worship.

WORSHIP INSISTS ON A HARMONIZING OF INNER ATTITUDES

Worship, of course, demands an awareness of God, for we cannot worship until we come into His Presence, but worship also involves a self-awareness. We do not enter into a trancelike state when we worship God, nor do the Scriptures call for a closing of the mind or the repression of our emotions when we come into God's Presence. As a matter of fact, one of the obvious contrasts between response to the demonic and response to the Divine is that the demonic prefers a mindlessness or trance, but God always demands an active mind and will. Relationship with God in worship is for the entire person—spirit, soul, and body—and we are invited to be willing and active participants in that experience.

It is possible, of course, for our soulish nature to so dominate the worship experience as to destroy it, for "God is Spirit, and those who worship Him must worship in spirit and truth" (John 4:24), but repression of the true nature of man is not the answer; a more workable answer is for each person to learn to harmonize his or her spirit with God's Spirit.

117

God seeks the worship not of robots but of redeemed persons whose wills have determined to worship Him. Our worship should never be independent of the Spirit of God but dependent upon the Holy Spirit. The mind of the worshipper needs to be submitted to the mind of God as revealed in God's Word; his emotions should blend with the moods of the Holy Spirit as evidenced in the work of God inwardly at the time of worship; and the spirit of the worshipper and the Spirit of God should flow in one channel unto the very heart of God. Self-awareness and Divine awareness need to blend as smoothly as a child flows lovingly into the arms of her mother without ever ceasing to be a child or attempting to replace the mother. For the moment, the two are one, although they are diversely different individuals.

There is equally a need to melt self-love and love for God in a worship experience. Some persons have expressed to me that they need a sense of complete worthlessness before they can worship. It seems to me that the Scriptures teach quite the opposite. Although self-love can become introspectively dangerous, the absence of any love of self makes it almost impossible to flow love out to another or to receive love from another. If the Word commands us to " 'love your neighbor as yourself' " (Mark 12:31), then loving God must require some measure of self-love.

Worship is not based on renunciation of honest inner attitudes; it is the expression to God of those attitudes. However, we need to learn to blend our estimation of ourselves with our appreciation for God, for the purpose of worship is to evidence our love for God, not our love for ourselves. Blending what we know we have become because of the active grace of God within us, with our deep respect, awe, admiration, and adoration of God, Who has effected such dynamic changes in us, is vital to worship.

Both self-negation and self-exaltation should be absent from a worship experience. Instead, our approach to God should be one of honest acceptance of who we are in life and who we are in Him. As the Bible says, "Let us draw near with a true heart in full assurance of faith, having our hearts sprinkled from an evil conscience and our bodies washed with pure water" (Hebrews 10:22).

WORSHIP IS A BLENDING OF MAN WITH GOD

Man's spirit and God's Spirit are never more uniquely blended than when we are in worship. Worship is an involvement between two persons, neither of whom totally controls the other. Worship effects an interaction of wills, emotions, attitudes, and concepts—both man's and God's—for worship is a love experience which, for the moment, blends two as though they were one.

John the beloved wrote, "I was in the Spirit on the Lord's Day, and I heard behind me a loud voice, as of a trumpet, saying, 'I am the Alpha and the Omega, the First and the Last' " (Revelation 1:10, 11). Out of this experience came the final book of the Bible. John and God so blended together that John could hear God's voice, see what God was doing, and even look into the future to behold the works of God that had not yet transpired. It all started in a worship experience.

All of Daniel's dreams and visions came out of worship experiences, and the prophets used to withdraw from other activities for lengthy seasons of worship in order to hear the voice of God for their people. Often it was difficult to distinguish between the man and his message, and frequently what was perceived by the seer was beyond his ability to express, but the vision and the message came as a natural outgrowth of man and God being blended together during a worship encounter.

It was out of deep experience that James wrote, "Draw near to God and He will draw near to you" (James 4:8). God does not separate Himself from us; it is we who separate ourselves from God, but when we set ourselves to worship, we retrace our steps back into the Presence of God and find Him eager to enter into an intimate and personal interaction with us.

As vital and valuable as this is, most of us have difficulty actually getting into a worship encounter with God. Perhaps that is why He has given us music as a channel of praise and worship, for music can lift us right out of ourselves and our circumstances and waft us into the realized Presence of God.

Now when He had taken the scroll, the four living creatures and the twenty-four elders fell down before the Lamb, each having a harp, and golden bowls full of incense, which are the prayers of the saints.
—Revelation 5:8

— 7 —

Worship Expands Through Music

The Sound of Music is far more than the title of an award-winning movie; it is a magnificent description of the American way of life. For us, music is everywhere. We hear the strains of music when shopping in a mall or eating in a restaurant. We drive our cars with the radios blaring, and we take portable radios or tape players with us to our favorite places of recreation. While we spend millions of dollars annually to "get away from it all," we do not allow ourselves to get away from music. Technologically we can have music anywhere and at any time, and psychologically we seem to crave the aesthetics of music as though it were a God-given drive or appetite. It is likely that some modern devotees listen to more music in a week than ancient monarchs heard during their entire reigns. Whether inevitably or by choice, music is undeniably a part of our lives.

MUSIC IN THE ANCIENT WORLD

The Western concept of music as an art, or even as a deluxe commodity of life, was utterly foreign to the ancient world. To the people in the years before David, music was an organic part of life, not an art form as such. For them, music was linked with a thousand bonds to all human concerns from birth to death. Perhaps our best modern illustration of this would be the way the black slaves of the South used music to enable themselves to survive the rigors of their lives. They sang to release their frustration, anger, and hopelessness; they sang to energize themselves for continued labor; they sang to maintain a sense of community in a lifestyle where they did not belong even to themselves. All pre-Davidic references to music must be understood from a similar perspective.

It seems that the main functions of music in the early times of biblical history were merrymaking, martial noisemaking,and incantation. During the period of the patriarchs and judges, merrymaking was the main function of music. All festivities were accompanied with music so that singing, dancing, and the playing of musical instruments became the heart of their festitivies.

The Interpreter's Dictionary of the Bible says, "Often the music barely exceeded the level of organized noise-making, especially when the purpose was to terrorize the enemy, as in Exodus 32:17, 18."[1] Much of their music was extemporaneous, such as the working songs of the harvesters (*see* Isaiah 16:10) and of the well-diggers (Numbers 21:17), and few, if any, of these songs were used on a repeated basis, much less passed on to others.

---

[1] *The Interpreter's Dictionary of the Bible*, Vol. 3. Nashville: Abingdon Press, 1962, p. 457.

DAVIDIC MUSIC

It was not until David's time that professional musicians appeared in the Bible. Before the establishment of the kingdom under Saul, it was the women who played a major part in the performance of music. As a matter of fact, from Jubal to David, music is basically described in a functionally neutral sense. Music-making was not religiously caused or primarily associated with worship. If there is one consistent stand in the Old Testament concerning music, it is that music is inseparable from all of life.

It was king David who seemed to bring music from daily living to the worship of Jehovah. Recognizing that the Levites who had been chosen to dismantle, carry, and re-erect the Tabernacle in the Wilderness no longer had any prescribed duties, although they were still considered as priests unto God, David created fresh portfolios for them. Of the 38,000 Levites chosen by David for Temple service following the return of Ark of the Covenant to Jerusalem, 4,000 of them were trained to be musicians before the Lord. David had a massed choir and a large orchestra that he divided into twenty-four courses so that music could be played and sung before the Ark twenty-four hours a day. David, who had written the words "He who keeps you will not slumber. Behold, He who keeps Israel Shall neither slumber nor sleep" (Psalm 121:3, 4), felt assured that God would enjoy the praise of music as much at 3:00 A.M. as at noon.

David put these musicians under three separate leaders—Heman, Asaph, and Ethan—perhaps providing for different styles of music; and he also invented and constructed instruments to be used in God's service.

He wrote much of the music that was sung before the Lord, and he seemed to have passed some of his musicological skills on to his son, for we are told that Solomon wrote 1,009 songs during his reign.

This was a transition to bring music from the secular to the sacred world, but all music of the Temple, regardless of the period, was nothing more than an accessory to the sacrificial ritual. We do know that the sacrifices remained forever central to the worship in the Temple, and music was a part of it. Just how David wove music into the sacrificial system is unknown, for this knowledge went to the grave with the Levites, who refused to divulge their secrets.

MUSIC IS INTRINSIC TO THE BELIEVER

It was no less a personage than Paul the apostle who taught us that music belongs to the essential nature of a Christian. He wrote to the church at Ephesus, "And do not be drunk with wine, in which is dissipation; but be filled with the Spirit, speaking to one another in psalms and hymns and spiritual songs, singing and making melody in your heart to the Lord" (Ephesians 5:18, 19). Paul was convinced that the point of overflow for the Spirit is singing, and he suggested that the Spirit would energize us to sing *psalms*—singing the Scriptures; *hymns*—musical poems about God, sung to God; and *spiritual songs*—or, as the Greek implies, extemporaneously composed musical numbers expressing ecstasy.

Paul equated the Presence of the Spirit with music in the believer, but when he wrote to those in Colossae, he suggested that this inner melody was a sign of being

126

filled with God's Word. "Let the word of Christ dwell in you richly in all wisdom," he wrote, "teaching and admonishing one another in psalms and hymns and spiritual songs, singing with grace in your hearts to the Lord" (Colossians 3:16). Here Paul said that beyond being an exuberant overflow of the Spirit within us, singing can be a teaching and learning experience, and that singing admonishes, encourages, edifies, and exhorts the Body of Christ. How vital, then, is that portion of our gathering together that is set aside for congregational singing. In many cases it contributes more to the encouragement of the believers than does any other portion of the service. Music, especially congregational singing, is a forceful element in worship.

It has often been said that we learn more doctrine from the hymnbook than from the Bible, for singing is a more powerful teaching tool than preaching. Furthermore, I have heard repeated testimonies of persons who have been drawn from sin to the Savior by the message and emotional impact of a song. The singing that will make such an impact upon the listener cannot be a mere performance; it will be a song that is sung "to the Lord" with accompanying "grace in your hearts." It is the melodious flow of God's Spirit through our spirits that becomes such a force for godliness.

To Paul, it seemed impossible to be filled with the Spirit and the Word of God without also being filled with song, for the Spirit is a singing Spirit, and God's Word is our hymnbook. God's Presence and His precepts stir such inward rejoicing that only singing can release it. Paul was more than propounding a theory; he was writing from experience, for some years prior to this letter, he and Silas, while bound in stocks in the inner dungeon there at Philippi, had found both emotional and physical release in singing. Paul knew that the Spirit does not sing only in cheerful, happy circumstances, but that the song of the Spirit is consistent in spite of our situation in life.

Frankly, we need the inner song of the Spirit more in harsh circumstances than in pleasant ones, for song renews faith and courage in the midst of adversity. Song joins us in fellowship with God and others and brings us back to a God-consciousness. Singing can give us endurance spiritually, emotionally, and physically. How marvelous it is that God's Spirit within us is a singing Spirit.

Historically, Christianity is the "singing religion." The hymns of Luther, sung in counterpoint by whole congregations, helped carry his message over central Europe, and the great revival in Wales was a singing revival, echoing throughout the mining villages. The Wesleys knew the power and inspiration that came from the hymn-singing of vast throngs, and far more of us have sung Charles Wesley's hymns than have ever read John Wesley's sermons. The evangelist Dwight L. Moody, with the musical ministry of Ira D. Sankey, moved two continents for God. Frequently Sankey would compose a closing hymn while Moody was preaching, and then sing it for the altar call.

Our generation has learned the power of singing in the vast Billy Graham crusades, and the great singing concerts of gospel artists have thrilled thousands of people. As a matter of fact, Church history records that any group that ruled out music as a part of worship had a very short survival span. The Spirit within us must sing!

Music is, indeed, intrinsic to the believer. We have a song within us—a song born of the Holy Spirit. We need not go through life with a Sony Walkman and earphones, for our music is within us, not without us. Those who have not surrendered their lives to Christ Jesus must depend upon an outside stimulus for their musical inspiration, but Christians have a song deep in their own spirit, and a Savior Who is the consistent theme of that song. The overflow of our spiritual joy explodes into song, and we are comforted, unified, and motivated by great gospel singing. The dirges of our slavery in sin have been exchanged for the songs of the redeemed. As one songwriter put it:

> I sing because I'm happy;
> I sing because I'm free;
> For His eye is on the sparrow,
> And I know He watches me.[1]

MUSIC, PER SE, IS NOT WORSHIP

Worship predates music, for Adam worshipped God in the garden of Eden, although music is not mentioned until the birth of Jubal (*see* Genesis 4:21), and even king David kept music as subsidiary to worship. This very fact establishes the truth that music in itself is not worship. No musical instrument is "an instrument of worship"; it may assist the musician in his worship, but

---

[1] "His Eye Is On the Sparrow." Homer A. Rodeheaver, owner, © 1934).

worship cannot be mechanical or inanimate. Worship is a person's spirit responding to God's Spirit, not a horn sounding musical tones throughout an auditorium. The same principle pertains to choir anthems, orchestral presentations, solos, or ensemble vocal songs sung at Christian gatherings. These musical offerings *can be* worship, but they are not necessarily expressions of worship unto God. Far too frequently they are artistic performances that draw more attention to the musician(s) than to God Himself.

Singing slow choruses or songs is not worship, although some songleaders seem to feel that the difference between praise and worship is the tempo used in singing. Singing in the minor key, or singing Jewish melodies, is not worship either. Tempo, pitch, key, style, or mode do not establish worship, for musicological skills are not, in themselves, worship skills.

Failure to recognize this leads congregations into confusion. If we say that music is worship, we will devastate those who are not "musical"; we will rule out the great portions of our congregations who have little, if any, musical skill, and will direct them to seek to worship by identification with those who can exhibit musical abilities. But worship by identification is an impossibility; worship demands participation. Sitting in the pew listening to the music is not a worship experience. Worship requires an involvement of persons with their God. It is, of course, possible to get involved with God in worship while listening to a musical presentation, but it is equally possible to enjoy the music in our souls without ever responding to God in our spirits.

Currently it is popular to upgrade the title of the song leader to that of "worship leader," as though worship could actually be led, and we refer to the time reserved for congregational singing as "worship time." These designations tend to reduce our concept of worship to that of music. Perhaps worship will occur while the congregation is singing; then again, it may not. Just leading people in singing does not mean that we are leading worship, for worship cannot occur until there is a consciousness of being in the Presence of God; and that may come during the singing, or the giving, or the praying, or the preaching of the Word. Other times, nothing that occurs in a church service provokes the worship of the congregation. Frankly, the most any of us can do is lead people. If we lead them to God, they will worship; but if we seek to lead them into an exercise of worship, we will destroy any possibility of their having a worship experience with God, for worship cannot be led—worship is response to God in a one-to-one relationship, and a third party in the middle hinders, rather than helps, the experience.

It has become a common introduction to say, "The choir will now worship the Lord in song"—which could be true, for some do, although many do not—but, again, we are equating song with worship. To make music synonymous with worship is to deprive Christians of discovering worship. Worship is far more than melody; it is love responding to love—or, better still, two lovers responding to each other. Worship requires an awareness of God's Presence, and music may create that awareness, or may easily detract from it.

Worship is an expression of God's majesty and nature

from the spirit of a redeemed one to God Himself. Unfortunately, much music is more involved with the believer than with God. Singing that produces introspection will prevent worship rather than channel it, for worship demands God-consciousness, not self-consciousness. The songs in which "I," "we," "us," and "they" are exalted do not help direct us into worship; those which exalt God the Father, God the Son, and God the Holy Spirit are the ones that inspire our worship. Although my musical ministry is now very dated, it appears to me that a large percentage of current religious music makes at best only a perfunctory reference to God. Perhaps this is done to make the music more commercial, but it makes it far less vital as a channel for worship. We do not worship ideologies, emotions, experiences, or abstract concepts of God; we worship Jesus, and we need to sing music that makes His name glorious!

Music, however religious it may sound, is not inherently worship. If it were, we could play a record or a tape and call that "worship." If music is worship, then worship can be composed, performed, led, and choreographed, but all worshippers know that this is not possible, for the moment we reduce the expression of love to a science, we have destroyed the love. Worship is not a science that inflexibly follows rules and laws of nature; there is something very abstract about worship, for worship is persons responding to the Person of Christ, and this will not follow formulas, nor can we predetermine how it is going to express itself at any given time.

MUSIC MAY BE INSEPARABLE
FROM WORSHIP

The four living creatures and the twenty-four elders not only had harps in their hands, but "they sang a new song" (Revelation 5:9). Again and again when we view worship in heaven, we see that the worshippers burst forth into song as though singing and worshipping were almost inseparable. Deep emotional feelings do not release themselves freely in mere words, but song has consistently proved to be a very practical method of expressing love, tenderness, and commitment.

Furthermore, music can set the scene for worship. When God told Samuel of His intention to accede to Israel's demand for a king, He sent for Saul to receive this kingly anointing. At the end of the special banquet, when Saul learned that he was God's choice for king over Israel, he was incredulous and insisted that he was not qualified for such a position. Samuel told him to return to his father's home, but also told him that on the way home he would " 'meet a group of prophets coming down from the high place with a stringed instrument, a tambourine, a flute, and a harp before them; and they will be prophesying. Then the Spirit of the Lord will come upon you, and you will prophesy with them and be turned into another man' " (1 Samuel 10:5, 6). This prophetic word was fulfilled to the letter, and young Saul not only found himself joining in the musical expression of praise, worship, and magnification of God, but also found an inner transformation taking place. He was, indeed, changed into another man.

We need to remind ourselves that the person who comes to church is seldom a worshipper; he is a person who needs to be changed into a worshipper. The individual who walks into the church building has his mind on natural things. His emotions are seldom stirred toward God, and very often he is actually in an emotionally low state. He has come to church to worship, but he needs something to stimulate him to worship. God used music to transform Saul, and nothing has yet surpassed music for effectiveness in doing this. Architecture and vestments may produce a feeling of wonder and awe, but music induces a response of worship unto God.

The world has long used music to affect behavior. Grocery stores control our shopping time with the music played over the loudspeakers. Doctors use music as therapy for many disorders, and the entertainment media sets the desired mood with both introductory and intermittent music. Even farmers have learned to use music to increase milk and egg production. Music has great power to affect behavior.

The church needs to learn to use introductory music to set the scene for worship as well as to use it as a channel for expressing that worship. Properly used, music can reach out and grab the minds of those present and turn them toward God. The musicians in the house of the Lord can stir religious fervor and desire even before the service begins. This introductory music can actually be a call to worship, for it can give people something with which to identify initially before trying to get them to be participants. The very mood of the music can "set the stage" for the nature of the message which is to follow.

MUSIC CAN UNITE WORSHIPPERS

The thirty-fourth Psalm was written when David was at one of the lowest moments in his life. He had fled from angry Saul, was responsible for the death of the priests at Nob, had joined the Philistine army—only to be so suspected that he had to pretend he had lost his mind in order to escape with his life—and he finally had taken refuge in the cave of Adullam. While he was there in hiding, his pity party was continually interrupted until he found himself surrounded by some four hundred men who were equally in distress, in debt, or discontented. In the eyes of king Saul, all of them were outlaws. One can only guess at the gloom, discouragement, and anxiety that filled Adullam's cave.

Perhaps David could have maintained leadership by regularly polishing Goliath's sword, which he had secured from the priests, but he felt too much like a failure to speak of past successes. Instead, he composed this Psalm and taught these men to sing, "I will bless the Lord . . . My soul shall make its boast in the Lord. . . . Oh, magnify the Lord with me, And let us exalt His name together" (Psalm 34:1-3). Something happened when these men began to sing together. This rag-tag gang of displaced men found themselves merged into a mighty fighting unit that Saul was never able to conquer. The names of many of these men appear in the listing of "David's mighty men" after the kingdom was secure. What David could not have accomplished with a sword, he gloriously produced with his harp. Music united them.

We may not have quite the same spectrum of persons in our churches on Sunday, but no two persons in the pews come from the same background, set of circumstances, or situations in life. Because of this diversity, united action is difficult, for the differences are greater than the similarities. Something is needed to weave these into one piece of cloth, and music—especially congregational singing—performs this task more perfectly than any other activity in which we could engage. Singing blends personalities together, for music is a powerful uniting force. The military learned this long ago. Martial bands parading on Main Street can motivate young men to sign up for military service, and fatiguing marches are made more bearable with singing in cadence. Political conventions use music artfully, and even ballparks install costly organs to help unite the attendants into rooting fans. They have learned something of the unifying power of music.

How often have I seen mixed congregations in the unfamiliar surroundings of a convention hall brought into a worshipping unit by little more than good congregational singing. The strains of "All Hail the Power of Jesus' Name" or "Hallelujah" unify both people and action.

MUSIC CAN SHELTER WORSHIPPERS

When God instructed Moses to construct the Tabernacle in the Wilderness as a place where the Israelites could worship, He made provision for a sheltering wall of white linen seven and one-half feet tall to be erected around the entire Outer Court. This served to separate the secular from the sacred; to protect the worshipper from the prying eyes of the neighbors; and, most importantly, to shut the worshipper in with God.

Everything his eyes could see reminded him of God and the Divine provision for approaching God. There was nothing distracting in the Outer Court, for this linen wall cut off all visual contact with the outside world.

The music of the Church should function much like this linen wall. We all come to church with minds crowded with the activities and business of the day, and merely sitting in pews surrounded by architecture that has religious implications is not sufficient to fasten our minds on spiritual things. Christ-centered music that is played, sung, and participated in can form a barrier to intruding thought patterns and so focus our attention upon the Lord Jesus Christ as to completely shut us in with God for a season.

Proper music gently "herds" us into one fold and then builds a protective wall around us. Everything that occupies our minds draws attention to God and His provision for approaching Him. We actually sing ourselves out of the natural realm into the spiritual, and the things of the secular world disappear from our vision as we look into the sacred realm of the Presence of God. Religion has consistently sought to build this protective fence with doctrine, creed, and ritual, but music is both faster and far more effective, for the worshipper gets invovled mentally, emotionally, and spiritually with his singing, whereas he tends merely to relate abstractly to doctrine and ritual. If more pastors realized the cloistering power of congregational singing, they would enlarge the period dedicated to singing instead of constantly encroaching upon that time for other religious activities. Just as there is nothing gained in giving a sales pitch until we have a prospective customer, so there is no sense in trying to worship until we have contacted God, and singing is among the finest methods of coming into His Presence.

MUSIC CAN RELEASE THE EMOTIONS

That we are emotional creatures goes without saying, but that we frequently find it difficult to express our true feelings is equally obvious. Often the price of true expression is too high, so we say what we think our peers want us to say. But unexpressed emotion becomes repressed emotion, and the habit of "gunnysacking" true feelings can produce very negative side effects, not the least of which is the inability to express emotion at all.

Paul and Silas in the Philippian jail (*see* Acts 16) certainly had pent-up emotions. They had been illegally arrested, beaten, imprisoned, and bound in stocks in the inner dungeon. If they didn't have negative emotions they must have been psycho cases. It's easy to imagine that as their stirred emotions began to turn to self-pity, one suggested to the other that perhaps they ought to sing for a while. Before long the feelings of injustice and unfairness gave way to praise unto the Lord, and God opened the prison to release them. Song was the vehicle that took them from wrath to worship, and so it can be for us.

The pent-up emotions in the pews in any given service are both varied and buried, but song can release these feelings in praise and adoration. Until our latent emotions are discharged, true worship is probably impossible, for expressions of love and adoration are difficult to release through emotions of anxiety and frustration. When I was a boy, we used to sing a chorus that I did not understand very well, but now that several decades have passed, I understand its poignant message:

> Sing the blues away;
> Night will turn to day;
> If we'll sing, and smile, and pray,
> We'll drive the blues away.

Many years ago I attended a denominational convention that was filled with danger. A seemingly insurmountable obstacle had arisen that threatened to split that great body of believers into two separate organizations. Most members accepted as a foregone conclusion that the separation was inevitable. What they had not reckoned with was the wisdom of the aged moderator who presided over the sessions. When he walked onto the dais, he brought with him a former classmate of mine, a man with a lyric tenor voice that could almost move the Rock of Gibraltar with his singing. Every time the discussion became dangerously heated with emotion, the moderator would call upon this vocalist to "favor us with a song." Wisely, the man always chose a well-known number, and he sang all the verses to the song. Somewhere in the song the delegates got so involved that they joined the final chorus, and in their singing, discharged their emotions to the place that getting the discussion going again was sometimes difficult.

By use of much singing, the moderator successfully defused the emotional aspect of the issue and kept the delegates to the facts. Without the intense feeling, the facts soon became manageable, and the split was prevented. Good, anointed, Christ-exalting music did more to preserve the denominational structure than did the multitude of committee sessions that had preceded the convention. Sometimes our hearts are so heated that our heads are clouded; music can bring us back to a place of clarity.

MUSIC GIVES VOCABULARY TO WORSHIP

Most people—especially men—have difficulty in releasing emotions publicly. Song, especially united singing, can be a crutch as well as a vehicle to assist them in expressing their feelings. To ask a group of men to stand and publicly say, "Jesus, I love You," may very well threaten them into silence, but to ask them to sing a verse of "My Jesus, I Love Thee" gives them an opportunity as well as a vehicle through which they can vocalize their devotion to Christ Jesus.

To direct a congregation to stand and say "Hallelujah" ten consecutive times will create an uneasiness among them, but to ask them to join together in singing "Hallelujah" will be a pleasant experience for them, even though in singing that chorus they will say "Hallelujah" ten times. The singing gives a reason for the repetition, and the music becomes a vehicle for saying the word differently each time.

One of the beauties of the old hymns is that others who have come into worship experiences have set to music their vocabularies of worship, and we can sing with them and worship with their language. Frequently their way of expression enlarges both our concept of God and our capacity to respond to God.

Singing our response to God has the double impact of enabling all of us to say the same thing at the same time. In singing, we both hear and speak the same words together, which reinforces the concept as well as the emotions that are released in the song. Singing enables us to have a double response to God because the mind is involved with the thought being sung and with hearing what is being sung.

The singing of the four living creatures and the twenty-four elders in Revelation chapter five not only released attitudes; it made positive declarations. Their song gave vocabulary to:

God's worthiness and rights—" 'You are worthy to take the scroll, And to open its seals' " (verse 9).

God's redemption and restoration of mankind—" 'For You were slain, And have redeemed us to God by Your blood' " (verse 9).

Our exaltation and relationship to God—" 'And have made us kings and priests to our God; And we shall reign on the earth' " (verse 10).

Feeling is fine, but being able to say something worthwhile in the midst of that feeling is even better. Music gives vocabulary to our thoughts during worship and may greatly enlarge our concepts of God as well in our singing of someone else's thoughts.

MUSIC CAN BE A WORSHIP-CHANNEL

Worship is the communion of the spirit with God, but music is a glorious channel for that communication. Music can be like a private phone line from man to God. It can be a clear channel through which we "broadcast" our worship toward heaven. It can be like a jet plane that transports us from earth to heaven. Music can be so much a part of our worship as to become inseparable from it. I am convinced that if we removed all music from our

141

public gatherings, worship would become stilted and would soon cease.

It is far less the quality of the music than the content of that music that makes it so vital in worship. Although we should always seek excellence in what we offer unto God as an act of worship, we need not wait for technical perfection before singing with grace in our hearts unto the Lord. It is far more important that what we sing makes us aware of God's Presence and makes God aware of our love and adoration. Whether expressed melodiously or verbally, worship speaks *to* God *of* God.

Then I looked, and I heard the voice of many angels around the throne, the living creatures, and the elders; and the number of them was ten thousand times ten thousand, and thousands of thousands, saying with a loud voice: "Worthy is the Lamb who was slain To receive power and riches and wisdom, And strength and honor and glory and blessing!"

—Revelation 5:11, 12

— 8 —

Worship Speaks *To* God *Of* God

If special coaching is needed to teach people how to respond when being presented to the Queen of England or the President of the United States, it is likelv that some instruction is germane for those who are to come before God Himself. What is the correct way to address God? What should and should not be said when in His Presence? Is there one style of vocabulary that is more acceptable than another? Is King James English better than the English of commerce? Whether or not we like to admit it, some or all of these questions have assailed us at one time or another.

Nothing in life can tie our tongues so rapidly and so completely as being introduced to a celebrity. While we await the introduction, our minds are filled with words of admiration and praise that we want to express; but the moment we have that personal audience, our minds go blank. Doesn't the same thing happen to us when we find ourselves in the Presence of the Almighty?

Unquestionably, the attitude of a person being presented to a dignitary is of prime importance, for attitudes govern actions. Worship, of course, begins as an attitude, but worship is more than a mere attitude; it is an attitude positively expressed to God, and it is the expressing of that attitude that so often gives us difficulty, for it is our deepest thoughts and strongest feelings that defy true expression with our limited vocabulary.

WORDS ARE IMPORTANT TO GOD

After much pleading with Israel, the prophet Hosea concluded his book by crying, "O Israel, return to the Lord your God . . . Take words with you, and return to the Lord. Say to Him, '. . . we will offer the sacrifices of our lips' " (Hosea 14:1, 2). The prophet was convinced that changed actions were insufficient; the people needed to come before the Lord with proper words of confession, consecration, praise, and worship. When he said, " 'We will offer the *sacrifices* of our lips,' " Hosea used a Hebrew word that literally means "bull calves." He felt that proper communication with God was comparable to the offering of a living animal as a sacrifice to initiate reconciliation with God. They needed to get back on speaking terms with God.

The book of Hebrews carries this thought a step further by saying, "Therefore by Him let us continually offer the sacrifice of praise to God, that is, the fruit of our lips, giving thanks to His name" (Hebrews 13:15). While Christ has become the sacrificial Lamb for time and eternity, we need to express our submission and worship unto God on a continual basis, and the words of our mouth become the acceptable sacrifice of conciliation in the New Testament.

David understood the use of words in expressing his worship to God, for he wrote, "Let the words of my mouth and the meditation of my heart Be acceptable in Your sight, O Lord, my strength and my redeemer" (Psalm 19:14). He wanted a right heart attitude, but he also wanted to express that attitude in a way that would be acceptable and pleasing to God. David's concept that the words he spoke to God were acts of worship is further illustrated when he said, "Let my prayer be set before You as incense, The lifting up of my hands as the evening sacrifice. Set a guard, O Lord, over my mouth; Keep watch over the door of my lips" (Psalm 141:2, 3). David, who was not a priest, could not offer incense or sacrifices to the Lord, but he could communicate with the Lord so expressively that he dared liken it to the worship of the Tabernacle.

SOURCES FOR A WORSHIP VOCABULARY

Since words addressed to God in times of worship are akin to the rituals of worship in the Temple, we do well to choose our words carefully so as to worship God reverently, honestly, and devotionally, for the sacrificial animals were the best of the flock, and the incense was compounded to a Divine formula. Unfortunately, however, we often have a very limited store of worship words in our normal vocabulary, for the language of commerce is almost useless in expressing love and devotion, and even the speech of the collegian may prove inefficient in communicating adoration and praise to God. Just as the computer student or the pilot in training

147

must learn a fresh vocabulary in order to communicate in his new field of endeavor, so worshippers often find it necessary to develop a vocabulary that becomes expressive of their attitudes toward God.

The richest source for such a vocabulary is, obviously, the Word of God, especially the Psalms and the book of Revelation. The Psalter is our hymnbook, and it is full of words that extol God and release our inner feelings about God. It is here that we learn phrases such as "I love the Lord, because . . ."; "I will extol You, O Lord"; "Oh, come, let us worship and bow down"; "Bless the Lord, O my soul"; "I will be glad and rejoice in Your mercy"; and several hundred other words and phrases that lift our spirits to God. The very reading aloud of the Psalms can become an act of worship, for there the human soul can find words to express virtually every emotion that is common to mankind. He who desires to become a worshipper would do well to familiarize himself with the Psalms, for they are vibrant expressions of the soul.

Because there is such vivid description given of the various worship groups in the book of Revelation, we can also glean many words that express worship from this book. We've already seen how powerful the word "worthy" is in heaven's worship, and it is this book that records such good use of "amen" and "hallelujah." From it we learn that blessing, honor, glory, wisdom, thanksgiving, power, and might are given to God as acts of worship. This last book of the Bible also gives us some beautiful songs and anthems that greatly enlarge our worship vocabularies. It should be evident to all of us that words of worship that are used in heaven will automatically be correct words to use in our worship here on the earth. That's what makes this sixty-sixth book of the Bible such a valuable textbook for worshippers.

While the Psalms and Revelation may have more worship language per page, the whole Bible is a rich source for our worship vocabulary. The responses of Abraham, Jacob, Moses, Samuel, the prophets, and others when they were in communication with God are rich sources for enlarging our worship vocabulary. So great was Moses' song of deliverance that it is combined with the song of the Lamb, and it is sung in heaven by the redeemed.

We must, of course, realize that the Bible is more than a worship thesaurus; it is God's revelation of Himself. The more we know God and know about God, the easier it will be to worship Him. The Old Testament saints didn't seek to tell God what they thought He wanted to hear; they told him what was deep in their hearts, and God accepted it as worship, for God prefers a truthful expression of a wrong attitude over a deceitful flow of "worship" words. This is illustrated repeatedly in the Old Testament, and it was declared by Jesus to the woman at the well when He told her, " 'God is Spirit, and those who worship Him must worship in spirit and truth' " (John 4:24). Fortunately, the Bible is the source for both the right attitude and the right vocabulary.

Another rich source for a worship vocabulary is the hymns of the Church. Men and women who have come into worship experiences with God have left us their vocabularies in the poems we have set to music. Who hasn't risen worshipfully in expressing the deep feelings of the soul when singing "All Hail the Power of Jesus' Name" or "Crown Him With Many Crowns"? Our hearts have been filled with fervor as we have sung "The name of Jesus is so sweet" or "Blessed assurance, Jesus is mine." The songs may vary with different religious heritages, but the worship vocabulary we learn from singing them can greatly enrich our expression of worship.

Some years ago when the congregation I was pastoring was coming into a level of worship unknown to them before, my sister, Iverna Tompkins, who was our music director at the time, began searching the very old hymnals for songs that gave better expression of what we were currently experiencing than did the choruses we sang. She used these hymns as choir numbers. Not only did they give our congregation an awareness that what we were experiencing was not new—it only was new to us—but they greatly enlarged our capacity to express ourselves in the midst of our new relationship with God.

Charles Spurgeon, that great English divine of the last century, is credited with having told his ministerial students that they needed to know their hymnbooks as well as they knew their Bibles. Perhaps all of us need a better acquaintance with the worship vocabulary to be found in the songs of yesterday.

An additional fountain that flows with an abundance of worship vocabulary is the prayers of saints who really know God. The Bible has many such prayers on its pages, but so does the rich literature of the Church, both ancient and modern. I happily confess that I have learned many acceptable ways of expressing my inner devotion to God by listening carefully to the prayers of men who have an intimate contact with the Lord Jesus Christ. Just as a child learns language by listening to those around him speak, so, too, we may learn to speak the language of worship if we will consciously listen to those who have already learned to worship. The goal is not to mimic, but to master the art of expressing our inner attitudes to God Himself.

WORSHIP SPEAKS *TO* GOD

We are aware, of course, that words in themselves do not necessarily communicate. Words are only tools, and the skill of communication lies in how those tools are used. When traveling in non-English-speaking countries, I have met persons with a very limited knowledge of the English language who could communicate love and devotion most effectively. Their tone, touch, gestures, and facial expressions augmented their limited vocabulary so well that there could be no mistaking their message. One of the keys to their effectiveness is the way they narrow their communication to a single person. It becomes obvious that they are not talking to the world; they are talking to me, and somehow that intimacy draws me into the communication to the place where feeling overrides the words that are used (or even misused).

Worship demands the same sense of intimacy, or personal involvement, with the one being worshipped. Worship should not be directed "to whom it may concern"; worship of God must always be addressed *to* God. Back when television was exclusively black and white, a producer gave me a prudent piece of advice just before I faced the cameras for my first time. "Television is very personal," he said. "Forget about an audience of thousands of people, and visualize a solitary person sitting in a room watching the TV set; then talk to that one person."

Worship demands the same mind-set. Worship is the communication of one person with Almighty God, and it dare not be treated as a broadcast to a vast audience. Worship is not the immature response of young lovers who are in love with love rather than with each other. Worship flows out of a commitment to Christ Jesus that has produced a submitted life, a surrendered will, and a self-expression of love and devotion. This will not take the form of a "letter to the editor"; it will be a love letter to Jesus, for worship is a response to the Person of God, not to the principles of God. Worship so focuses its communicated thoughts upon the Lord that there is no mistaking Who the recipient actually is. It is far more than love professed—it is love poured out to God very much as Mary poured out the costly liquid nard upon the head and feet of Jesus.

When our spirits are focused upon the object of our worship, the method of expression that we use is incidental. We may communicate our worship through the prayer channel, or we may merely have a conversation with God while we go about our daily activities. Other times we may read or quote Scripture passages to God with a "that's the way I feel, too" postscript added. Sometimes worship can be communicated with gestures and body postures while meditating upon God, but whether we write Him a letter, sing Him a song, or read a Scripture portion to Him, the key to successful worship is to do it unto God Himself. As John was instructed, " 'Worship God!' " (Revelation 19:10). The Bible does not merely call us to worship; it commands us to worship God.

152

WORSHIP SPEAKS *OF* GOD

Worship requires us to speak to God, but so does prayer. Each demands a personal focus upon the Person of God. The fundamental difference between the two is that *prayer* speaks to God about ourselves, our needs, and our feelings, while *worship* speaks to God *of* God. Worship extols God, while prayer explains us to God. In worship, any reference to self is incidental. It is God Who is the subject, and release of our love, gratitude, and admiration is the intent.

Speaking *to* God *about* God is amply illustrated in the book of Revelation, where the song of the living creatures and the elders is totally concerned with Christ Jesus: " 'You are worthy . . . You were slain . . . [You] have redeemed us to God by Your blood . . . [You] have made us kings and priests to our God' " (5:9, 10). When the angels joined this select group, they also spoke to God of God by saying, " 'Worthy is the Lamb who was slain To receive power and riches and wisdom, And strength and honor and glory and blessing!' " (Revelation 5:12). In the next verse we are told that "every creature which is in heaven and on the earth and under the earth and such as are in the sea, and all that are in them, I heard saying: 'Blessing and honor and glory and power Be to Him who sits on the throne, And to the Lamb, forever and ever!' " (verse 13).

Every word uttered by this expanding group of worshippers was centered on God and the Lamb. Their exclamations became an extolling of the excellence of God. And so should our worship. We need to learn the value of telling God what He has told us about Himself, for, frankly, that is all we know about God. The language

153

of love consistently tells the object of that love how great he or she is, and amplifies the virtues of the individual. This is not the language of discovery or instruction; it is the language of attitude and feeling, and it fits beautifully into the expression of our worship.

This is consistent with worship in heaven, for we hear the angels decaring God's nature in saying, " 'Holy, holy, holy is the Lord of hosts; The whole earth is full of His glory!' " (Isaiah 6:3). While the theologian would speak of the essential nature of God as being omnipotence, omniscience, omnipresence, and eternity, the worshipper would rephrase that into more intimate words and would more likely tell God that His power is amazing, His understanding of every little detail in life is comforting, His Presence is to be found everywhere in the world, and His transcendence of all time is inconceivable. The very expressing back to God of our limited understanding of His attributes releases our spirits to worship One Who is so much greater than we are, and yet He invites us to come into His Presence to fellowship with Him.

The style, intensity, and attitude of our worship are often governed by our concepts of God's nature. After Moses had witnessed the wrath of God in the incident of the golden calf, he ascended Mount Sinai once again, carrying the two tables of stone he had cut as replacements for the tables on which God had written but which had been thrown down and broken. God met Moses on the mountain "and proclaimed the name of the Lord," or, more technically, God described His nature to Moses, for God has chosen to reveal His nature to us through various compound names He gives to Himself. The proclamation that God gave to Moses was

" 'The Lord, the Lord God, merciful and gracious, long-suffering, and abounding in goodness and truth, keeping mercy for thousands, forgiving iniquity and transgression and sin, by no means clearing the guilty. . . ' So Moses made haste and bowed his head toward the earth, and worshiped" (Exodus 34:6-8). The words that Moses used in expressing worship at this time were harmonious with what God had just told him.

Worship is a natural response to a revelation of God, and the expression of that worship will often take the form of reciting back to God, joyfully or devotedly, what we have learned of His nature. The mere recounting of what God told Moses would constitute a worship session for a worshipper, for worship is often released in rejoicing in God's mercy, grace, goodness, and truth; and Paul's declaration that Christ Jesus "became for us wisdom from God—and righteousness and sanctification and redemption" (1 Corinthians 1:30) can, of itself, be a grand expression of worship. When we are overwhelmed with our own inabilities, we can worship Christ in and for His abilities made available to us.

God's nature, as revealed in the Bible, is rounded and complete. He is everything we could ever need or desire, and when we come before Him in worship, we often express our concept of His absolute completeness by reciting back to Him what we have learned of His nature. It reinforces our awareness of God's sufficiency and releases our awareness that we are complete only in Him, for He has chosen to share His Divine nature with us, according to Peter: ". . . His divine power has given to us all things that pertain to life and godliness, through the knowledge of Him who called us by glory and virtue, by which have been given to us exceedingly great and precious promises, that through these you may be partakers of the divine nature, having escaped the corruption that is in the world through lust" (2 Peter 1:3, 4).

Beyond speaking of God's attributes and nature, worship often finds expression in speaking the names of God, for these are channels of God's self-revelation. How natural it seems to say to God, "Lord, You are my Shepherd, and I have no anxieties when I stay close to You," or "Lord, Your very Presence brings me into a peace I cannot find anywhere else." In our own way we are proclaiming both the name and the nature of the Lord, for He has revealed Himself to be *Jehovah-Ra-ah*, "the Lord our Shepherd," and *Jehovah-Shalom*, "the Lord our peace." Some find great release of inner worship in singing *"Jehovah-Jireh*, my Provider," for in declaring that name of the Lord, they enter into a fresh relationship with God.

Even with a very limited knowledge of our God, we can worship with the simple recitation of His name. All of us have experienced a release of worship in saying, "Jesus, O Jesus," or "Abba, Father," or "My Lord, I love You!" Isaiah seemed to realize this, for he wrote, "His name will be called Wonderful, Counselor, Mighty God, Everlasting Father, Prince of Peace" (Isaiah 9:6). What names—what a nature—what a God is He! Who of us has not cried out each of these names as an expression of wonder and worship?

Worship does indeed speak to God about God. It expresses what we know about God's attributes, nature, names, and character, and it often recounts His gracious

156

actions on our behalf. It extols God to the highest level of our concepts and capacity to communicate those thoughts. Neither our perception of God nor our proclamation to God need be perfect for worship to be glorious, for Paul himself admitted, ". . . we know in part and we prophesy in part," but he assured us that "when that which is perfect has come, then that which is in part will be done away" (1 Corinthians 13:9, 10). Here on the earth we are but imperfect students of worship, but in heaven we will worship as perfectly as the angels.

WORSHIP ALWAYS SAYS SOMETHING

Repeatedly in the book of Revelation, John said, "I heard saying . . ." in connection with worship, for worship is always the declaration of an inner devotion. The living creatures vocalize their worship, the elders express their worship, the angels speak worship, and the redeemed saints seen in heaven loudly proclaim their adoration of God in words of highest magnification. Worship in heaven says something, and that something is eulogy of God spoken to God.

In Revelation chapter five we hear the blessed heavenly beings "saying with a loud voice: 'Worthy is the Lamb who was slain To receive power and riches and wisdom, And strength and honor and glory and blessing!' " (verse 12). They are ascribing to God most of the things that we on earth desire from God. If we were to subtract these seven things from our petitions, there actually would be very little left for most of us to pray about, but in the worship of heaven, not one of the worshippers is asking for these things—they all are vocally declaring Christ's worthiness to possess everything.

157

The true key to worship is giving to God, not getting from God. It is not worship to ask God to bless us, and yet how regularly do we pray for God to bless our activities, bless our ministries, bless our everything! Similarly, we beseech God to honor His Word, honor His servant, honor us with His Presence, and so on, but in worship these things are conferred *upon* Christ, not conferred *by* Him.

In the worship recorded in chapter seven, the vast throng clothed in white robes cried out with a loud voice, " 'Salvation belongs to our God who sits on the throne, and to the Lamb' " (verse 10). It was a vocal acknowledgment that their very salvation was not truly possessed by them but was merely enjoyed by them. Salvation belongs to the Lord Who purposed it, purchased it, provided it, and perpetuates it. It is His salvation; we are the saved. Worship likes to proclaim God's ownership of the entire scheme of redemption.

When all the angels joined the rest of the worshippers, they, too, had something to say. Knowing God better than any of the redeemed could know Him, they cried, " 'Amen! Blessing and glory and wisdom, Thanksgiving and honor and power and might, Be to our God forever and ever. Amen' " (Revelation 7:12). This certainly is in harmony with scriptural precedent, for Moses proclaimed in his song, " 'Ascribe greatness to our God. He is the Rock, His work is perfect; For all His ways are justice, A God of truth and without injustice; Righteous and upright is He' " (Deuteronomy 32:3, 4), and David cried, "Ascribe strength to God . . . O God, You are more awesome than Your holy places" (Psalm 68:34, 35). Worship glorifies God in everything that it says and does.

At whatever point the expression or action begins to glorify the worshipper, it ceases to be worship of God.

In speaking to God of God, worship resembles a fiftieth wedding anniversary when all the children and grandchildren come together to celebrate the grand occasion by eulogizing, praising, and appreciating the mother and father who gave them a chance in this world. When we get to heaven, we will discover that worship is a celebration, but if we can discover it here on earth, we can enter into that celebration now and enjoy it into eternity as well as throughout all eternity.

After these things I looked, and behold, a great multitude which no one could number, of all nations, tribes, peoples, and tongues, standing before the throne and before the Lamb, clothed with white robes, with palm branches in their hands, and crying out with a loud voice, saying, "Salvation belongs to our God who sits on the throne, and to the Lamb!" And all the angels stood around the throne and the elders and the four living creatures, and fell on their faces before the throne and worshiped God . . .

—Revelation 7:9-11

— 9 —

Worship Is A Celebration

To maintain an attitude of true worship, we must cultivate an awareness that worship is the celebration of God. At least that is what worship is in heaven, and we must pattern our earthly response to God after the example that has been given to us in the Bible. Saints from antiquity into eternity have celebrated God in their worship experiences, and the picture given to us in the seventh chapter of Revelation is no exception. Everything that is being said and done is not only done unto God, but is performed as a commemoration of God and the Lamb. These heavenly worshippers are doing far more than eulogizing God; they are thoroughly enjoying God.

This may not be very religious, but it is very real. Like the Old Testament worship that was built around feasting, fellowshipping, and festivity, the worship in heaven is pictured as a delightful occasion that is enjoyed by both God and the worshippers. The solemnity of the worship does not overpower the enjoyment of the celebration in heaven, and it should not do so here on earth. We earthlings, who celebrate holidays, birthdays, wedding anniversaries, sports victories, and a host of other events, should have little difficulty enjoying worship if we can just see worship as a celebration on a much higher level.

THE CELEBRANTS

The worship we have examined in chapter five of the book of Revelation is limited to the four living creatures, the twenty-four elders, and the "many angels." Here in chapter seven, the number of celebrants has expanded into a "great multitude which no one could number, of all nations, tribes, peoples, and tongues, standing before the throne and before the Lamb . . ." (Revelation 7:9). This is not an exclusive group; it could not be more inclusive.

Some years ago, when I was writing my book titled *Heaven*, I was impressed with the gigantic dimensions given by John for the New Jerusalem, which will serve as the home for the saints. It will take a lot of redeemed ones to fill its streets, and since God is not a God of waste, I had to accept that far more persons have been redeemed through the ages than my mind had allowed. In seeking to calculate the number of redeemed who join the angels in the worship of God, John, who earlier had calculated up to 100 million, just admitted that the multitude was beyond the scope of any mere mortal to number.

Because most of us are quite parochial in our religious experiences, it is easy for us to believe that "our" church is the only true worshipping church, or that "my" denomination is the only worshipping denomination in America. John saw the facts as being far broader than our bigoted views. He saw a multitude of worshippers so numerous as to dwarf the combined totals of the attendance figures at all the football stadiums in America on New Year's Day.

This throne is not only multitudinous; it is interracial. John spoke of every political and linguistic division with which he was familiar, and declared that each had its representatives before the Throne, worshipping the Lamb. And yet, for all of this representation, there are no identifying characteristics mentioned. We do not read of "the black delegation," or of "the trade unions"; we don't even see a distinction being made between men and women. As I stated in chapter five, worship blends the worshippers together until the individual characteristics are lost in the process and are indistinguishable in the product.

I do not foresee heaven as being divided into denominational sectors, or believe that the affluent on earth will have a higher place in heaven than will the poor. Earthly distinctions disappear at the grave, and in God's Presence we are not known by the language we spoke on earth, the doctrine we embraced before entering heaven, or even the period of time during which we were born and later born again. Heaven reduces the redeemed to the common denominator of worshippers.

The flow of worship we saw coming from the angels and the living creatures of heaven is all but drowned out by the enthusiastic release of worship that pours from the recently arrived redeemed ones. The celebrants have great cause for their celebration, for this is their first encounter with their Redeemer, and all of their anxieties have been replaced with the full assurance that entering heaven brought to them. The emotional impact of this exchange is released in voluminous praise and worship of God.

THE PLACE OF CELEBRATION

Worshippers are redeemed persons who have finally met their Redeemer, and their worship is released in the presence of their saving God. John observed that this vast multitude of celebrants was "standing before the throne and before the Lamb" (Revelation 7:9). It is easy to forget that worship cannot be done anywhere we choose. The Old Testament abounds with demonstrations of this fact, for God prohibited the celebration of worship anywhere but in the place He had appointed. Even the properly prescribed rituals of worship were viewed as idolatrous if they were practiced anywhere other than the Tabernacle, and later, the Temple. The very erection of an altar away from the Tabernacle nearly triggered a civil war in the days of Joshua until it was proven that the altar in question was built for a memorial and not as a place to offer sacrifices.

Worship in heaven is offered before the Throne of God. It is when the celebrants are in the recognized Presence of the Almighty that worship pours forth, and so it is here on earth. We can worship only when we are in the Presence of God. We can praise from any position, because praise is what brings us into the Presence of God, but we can worship only after we touch God. It requires an awareness of God for our spirit to reach out to His Spirit in worship. This may, and should, happen when we are involved in the rituals and sacraments of the Church, but often it does not. Worship is not a response to religious activity; it is a response to a real Person—God.

Since worship is love responding to love, until love touches us we cannot respond in worship. The Bible declares and demonstrates God's love for us, but until there is a reception of that love, John 3:16 is academic rather than actual. Love ignored is ineffectual, love spurned is unfruitful, love embraced is transforming, but love returned is worship. This flow of love between the redeemed and their Redeemer will take place only when there is a consciousness of being together.

This awareness may occur during a public gathering of believers, or it may happen on the job, in the home, while driving a car, or, as is often the case with me, while flying in a plane. The heart of the believer can become the Throne of God when the eye of faith enables the person to see beyond the natural world and catch a glimpse of God involved in daily activities. Whenever there is an awareness of God, worship is a natural response.

Unfortunately, it often happens that the very activity that is designed to bring us into a worship experience prevents true worship by drawing attention away from God rather than to God. We never worship as long as we are looking at people or at ourselves. We worship only when we see God on the Throne and His Lamb by His side. The greater our awareness of the priest, pastor, singer, or ourself, the less chance there is for true worship, for worship is not a spectator sport; it is a participating response to the Presence of God.

The fact that worship is seen only before the Throne of God shows progression in the approach of the believers, for the pattern of heaven, unfolded in the Tabernacle in the Wilderness, places the Throne of God in the Holy of Holies—the innermost court of the entire Tabernacle. The approaching priest ministered at the Brazen Altar, the Laver, the Candlestick, the Table of Shewbread, and the Golden Altar of Incense before he finally stood before the Mercy Seat—the Throne of God—and even then there was a veil that separated him from the Throne.

Worship is not a one-step activity; it is the climax of preceding activities. We must learn to move from our natural lives into the Outer Court of God's provision and appropriate the work of the cross and the Word of God. Next we can step into the Presence of God as it is revealed by the light of the Holy Spirit, applied by the bread of His Presence, and responded to in the incense of our prayers and praises. Then, and only then, can we approach the Throne of God to worship with our whole hearts. The farther we live from God in the consciousness of our lives, the longer it takes us to come into a worship experience with Him. God is not worshipped in the Outer Court; He is served there. He is not really worshipped in the Inner Court, either; He is fellowshipped there. It is when we stand in His presence before the Throne of grace that worship can flow unhindered and unrestrained. This means that we must move beyond our physical senses—the Outer Court of life—and even rise above our emotional feelings—the Holy Place—to release our spiritual perceptions as worship in the Holy of Holies of our being. We are body, soul, and spirit, but we originate worship to God in our spirit.

THE CELEBRITY

Responding to a celebrity should be easy for anyone raised in the American culture. We love a celebrity! Whether he or she is an entertainment idol, a sports champion, a popular politician, or a current hero, we shower admiration, adoration, and affection on that person. From tickertape parades to festive banquets, we applaud his (or her) person, bask in his presence, and seek his autograph. We often exalt him to godlike stature in our adulation.

We know how to respond to a celebrity—unless that celebrity happens to be God, and then we respond as though we were attending a funeral. Perhaps we need to return to the empty tomb with Peter and John, or step into the upper room with the disciples while Jesus displays His wounds to Thomas. Worship should never be a mere memorial service; worship celebrates a living God, not a dead war hero.

Worshippers stand before a saving God, not a sentencing judge. Our sins were judged at Calvary in the Outer Court; our lives have been cleansed at the Laver, and we have been made partakers of the Divine nature at the Table of Shewbread. We have been invited and conducted into the Divine Presence, and ". . . having boldness to enter the Holiest by the blood of Jesus, by a new and living way which He consecrated for us, through the veil, that is, His flesh . . . let us draw near with a true heart in full assurance of faith, having our hearts sprinkled from an evil conscience and our bodies washed with pure water" (Hebrews 10:19, 20, 22). We do not dread to come into God's presence; we delight in coming to the Throne for festive worship.

It is possible, however, to get so caught up in the festivity as to forget the occasion for the party. Thousands of Christmas parties are conducted annually where Christ is not even mentioned, much less thought of. This can happen to worshippers as well. We can get so involved in the celebration as to forget Whom we are celebrating. Since the only acceptable object of our worship is God Himself, the celebration of worship must always keep God as the Celebrity.

As in all earthly celebrations, where there are lesser persons who often capture brief moments in the spotlight, so in our celebration we will have momentary consciousness of persons and things less than God. We will see personalities, programs, preaching, and religious practices, but these are not to be celebrated. They may become part of the celebration, but God, and God alone, is the Celebrity in worship. Nothing should draw attention away from Him; if anything does, it is out of order. No soloist, songleader, pastor, or preacher should ever step into the spotlight that belongs to God. They are valuable in helping to direct us in our worship celebration, but they are dangerous if they allow themselves to become the celebrity. Sometimes the fault lies with the worshipper rather than with the leader, for no matter how hard leaders may try to avoid being "front and center," if we focus our attention on them we have lost sight of the true Celebrity, and our worship of God can degenerate into hero worship of persons.

THE ADORNMENT OF THE CELEBRANTS

John observed that this innumerable host of worshippers were "clothed with white robes" (Revelation 7:9). This seems to indicate that there are vestments for worship—spiritual garments that are provided for worshippers. It is reminiscent of the story Jesus told in the Gospels about the wedding feast that provided special garments for the attendants. When a guest was discovered at the reception wearing his own garment, he was removed from the celebration. Just as a football player must wear the designated uniform if he intends to play in the game, so worshippers are expected to wear the vestments of white robes when they come before the Throne of God in worship.

That this is a spiritual figure of speech is clearly explained in the context, for John was told, " 'These are the ones who come out of the great tribulation, and washed their robes and made them white in the blood of the Lamb' " (Revelation 7:14). The garment speaks of the purity of the worshipper. No Old Testament priest dared to come into the Presence of God unwashed. He not only washed himself completely, but he paused at the Laver for self-inspection and further cleansing. No New Testament believer-priest should come into the Presence of God in a defiled condition, for God cannot have communion with a defiled person, but He has made ample provision for the cleansing of the redeemed.

The vestments of worshippers are lives made clean by the shed blood of God's Lamb, Jesus Christ. This imagery was first used by John in the third chapter of the book of Revelation in the promise to the overcoming believers in the Church at Sardis: " 'He who overcomes shall be clothed in white garments' " (verse 5). The robes are gifts given as awards to the overcomers. God is still calling for Christians to overcome the world rather than to be overcome by the world. The call of the Spirit through the apostle John needs to be heard and obeyed in our generation as much as in the early Church. John wrote, "Do not love the world or the things in the world. If anyone loves the world, the love of the Father is not in him. For all that is in the world—the lust of the flesh, the lust of the eyes, and the pride of life—is not of the Father but is of the world" (1 John 2:15, 16).

Toward the end of his account, John observed, "For the fine linen is the righteous acts of the saints" (Revelation 19:8). Worshippers are clothed in righteousness—a righteousness that has been conferred upon them by Christ. That this righteousness is necessary is obvious from the statement to the Church in Sardis: " 'They shall walk with me in white' " (Revelation 3:4). Walking with God calls for increased levels of righteousness and holiness. The more intimately we walk with God, the more God deals with intimate things in our lives. God wants to have a holy people who can enjoy a holy God.

White robes speak of the righteousness that has been given to us through Jesus Christ. In no way does this refer to the self-righteousness of our human works, soulish feelings, or religious pretenses. Isaiah quite accurately said, "We are all like an unclean thing, And all our righteousnesses are like filthy rags" (Isaiah 64:6). We do not make the robe; we merely receive it from Jesus and keep it clean by washing it when our daily walk soils it. The promise to the Christian is "If we confess our sins, He is faithful and just to forgive us our sins, and to cleanse us from all unrighteousness" (1 John 1:9).

The worship vestment is a gift, but its maintenance is a personal responsibility. We learn to come to God by way of the Word of God for cleansing from every daily defilement that would hinder our response to a holy God.

One of the great hindrances to a flow of worship while we are in the Presence of God is an awareness of inner defilement. The conscience within, and the devil without, whisper, "You have no right to worship God today. You did (or didn't) do . . . you thought . . . you said. . . ." If what we are looking at is sin, we should immediately confess it, but if it is only human unrighteousness, we need to remind ourselves that in God's Presence we are clothed with the righteousness of Christ. We will never be inherently worthy to worship God, but Christ has made us worthy. He has conferred His righteousness upon us to enable us to stand in the Presence of the Father with head held high, knowing that we have been accepted in Christ Jesus. We have been provided a vestment that gives us the right to stand before the Throne with believers of all ages and worship God in spirit and truth. There is no power in heaven or hell or on earth that can prevent us from worshipping when we are wearing the white robes of Christ's righteousness.

This concept of vestments for worshippers is seen not only in the books of the Law; the psalmist speaks of it in writing, "Let Your priests be clothed with righteousness, And let Your saints shout for joy" (Psalm 132:9). The coupling of righteousness with joy seems to unite the vestments with the festivity of worship. Isaiah saw much the same thing when he wrote the passage that Jesus read in His home-town synagogue and declared was fulfilled in their eyes: " 'The Spirit of the Lord God is upon Me, Because the Lord has anointed Me . . . [to give them] the garment of praise for the spirit of heaviness' " (Isaiah 61:1, 3).

The vestments of worshippers are garments of right-eousness and joyful praise. We are clothed not with solemnity but with rejoicing. The white robes are not meant to inhibit our joy, as a child's special "Sunday clothes" often do to him, but to help us in releasing that joy. They are more than a fancy uniform; they are a replacement for impurity and heaviness. Just as a sweatsuit releases a jogger for freedom of movement, so the white robes of righteousness and joy release the worshippers to unrestricted response in the midst of their festive celebration of God.

What a sight it must be to see such a vast multitude of people all clothed with similar garments of Christ's righteousness and our praise. In this respect there will be uniformity in heaven, for we will all wear these vestments.

THE CELEBRATION

Again and again, as John was conducted through heaven, he saw and heard worship being offered to God. A montage of these observations proves that heaven's worship is a festivity. John saw people marching in uniforms, shouting, and waving pompoms (7:9, 10). He saw the Temple opened for worship (11:19) and incense being offered on the Golden Altar (8:3). He heard instrumentalists (14:2; 15:2) and singers (14:3; 15:3), followed by more loud shouts of " 'Alleluia!' " (19:1). Praise was called for, not unlike the cheerleader calling for a cheer (19:5), and the response was as thunderous as a cascading waterfall (19:6).

The worship scenes concluded with the injunction " 'Let us be glad and rejoice and give Him glory' " (19:7). The Greek word John used for "be glad" is *chairo*. Dr. Strong defines this word as "to be cheerful—impersonal, especially as a salutation (on meeting

172

or parting); be glad; hail; rejoice."[1]

Just as the Hawaiians use the word "aloha" for both a greeting and a farewell, so the worshippers in heaven use "Be glad" as their enthusiastic introductory or parting remark. It certainly is to be preferred over our hypocritical greeting "How are you?" Heaven's worshippers aren't concerned with one another's health (for there is no sickness in heaven); they salute one another with a challenge to be cheerful, to rejoice in the Lord. Their communication is geared to keep their spirits high and their enthusiasm flowing, very much as the fans do at an exciting ball game.

The second challenge that comes from this multitude of worshippers is "Let us rejoice." The Greek word here is *agalliao*, which, according to Dr. Strong, means "to jump for joy; exult; be (exceeding) glad; rejoice (greatly)."[2] These worshippers seem unafraid to use body language in their worship of God, for we see them prostrate before God, waving palm branches, marching, singing, and playing musical instruments, and here they even challenge one another to "jump for joy." Worship in heaven is not all words—it is communication of deep inner feelings about God to God. Heaven's redeemed know that words by themselves are inefficient tools for this kind of communication, and that gestures, facial expressions, and bodily posture often communicate deep feelings more honestly and effectively than words alone.

---

[1] *Strong's Exhaustive Concordance of the Bible*—Greek Dictionary. Grand Rapids, Michigan: Baker Book House, reprinted 1977, p. 7.
[2] Strong, p. 77.

It is overdue for the saints on earth to recognize this reality. We, who use body language even when talking on the telephone, try to worship God stony-faced and immobile, but it is often as inadequate a communication as a child's forced apology: the words are right, but they don't communicate the true feelings. Body language is natural to all of us—it preceded speech in our lives. God is not anti-human; He made us human beings, and He comfortably relates to us as we are. Body language is no threat to God, but it is a tremendous aid to us when we come into His Presence.

It is almost impossible to read John's description of the worship he saw in heaven without coming to the conclusion that worship, offered in God's Presence, is a celebration of God—a festivity. Having told us that the worshippers were all dressed alike (could this be the cheering section wearing the school colors?), John said that they were holding "palm branches in their hands" (Revelation 7:9). Of course our minds go back to the triumphal entry of Christ into Jerusalem, when the jubilant multitude tore fronds from the palm trees and waved them enthusiastically as they cried, " 'Hosanna! Blessed is He who comes in the name of the Lord!' " (Mark 11:9).

If John were writing this book today, I wonder if he might use the term "pompoms," for we Americans no longer wave palm fronds at our celebrations— we prefer colorful pompoms. What a sight it would be to see this vast aggregation of people from all over the world, dressed in heaven's colors and waving pompoms like a cheering section at a football game. It would certainly be a contrast to most worship services to which we have become accustomed in our churches here on earth.

As if this would not be disturbing enough to the solemnity of worship, John said that these celebrants were "crying out with a loud voice" (Revelation 7:10). Every time we see worship in heaven, there seems to be this loud shouting and proclamation of the virtues and graces of our God. In this book of Revelation, worship begins with the four living creatures, who are later joined by the twenty-four elders, who in turn are joined by "many angels." This is enlarged to the incalculable host of redeemed persons, and later we are told that "all the angels" joined in the worship. Interestingly enough, on each occasion we are told that they shouted with "a loud voice." Certainly the volume was not necessary for communication with God, for they were standing before the Throne of God. The loudness was necessary to honestly release the emotion that had built up inside the worshippers. While admitting that there is a place for quietness in worship, integrity compels us to also admit that there is a time for exuberant and loud praising of God, for truth in worship is vital, and quietness is not always an honest expression of the way we feel when we sense the Presence of God.

Pompoms (or palm branches) and shouting speak of excitement. Isn't it overdue for God's Church on earth to begin to get excited about God? What's wrong with waving some banners or flags as an expression of our love for God? If we could see the extent of God's grace working in our lives, wouldn't that elicit a shout? If we could be as certain of entering heaven as those who had actually arrived, wouldn't the release of the pent-up emotion almost demand some pompom waving?

Oh, yes! Worship is indeed a celebration when it is done as they do it in heaven. Visualize these worshippers in heaven as being seated in a giant stadium. Can you see Paul and Peter acting as cheerleaders for the crowd? "Rejoice in the Lord always. Again I will say, rejoice!" (Philippians 4:4), Paul shouts over the megaphone.

"Be glad with exceeding joy" (1 Peter 4:13), Peter challenges as he and Paul prepare to lead these pompom-waving fans in a cheer.

"Give me a *J!*" they cry. "Give me an *E!* Give me an *S-U-S!* Jesus! Jesus! JESUS!"

Listen to the cheering. Look across the stadium at the thousands of colorful pompoms being waved in excitement against the background of the white robes. Listen to the bands, and watch the people, leap, jump, dance, wave their hands, and in a hundred different ways express their joy and enthusiasm. This is jubilee! This is a festival. They are celebrating God! Oh, how weak and puny our little liturgies of worship must seem when they are compared to the way God is accustomed to being worshipped in heaven.

THE CELESTIAL COMMENDATION

For those to whom this form of worship seems improper and irreligious, the response to God of these worshippers must be a conundrum, since God does not restrict, restrain, or reprove them for any of their actions. Instead, God rewards them in seven specific ways, as the elder explained to John in Revelation 7:13-17.

" 'Therefore they are before the throne of God, and serve Him day and night in His temple,' " John was told (verse 15). The first proof of God's commendation of their worship is their being granted to come before the Throne. They are rewarded with the Presence of God. Praise can bring us into the Presence of God, but worship allows us to remain in that Presence. Worship opens a permanent pathway that allows us to go into and come back out of God's realized Presence.

The second commendation is the assurance that these worshippers " '. . . serve Him day and night in His temple' " (verse 15). On earth we have thousands of redeemed persons who are working *for* the Lord, and hundreds who are serving *with* the Lord, but worshippers serve the Lord Himself. The full thrust of worship is unto God; it is serving God directly rather than through service to people. It is handing something directly to God instead of "to the least of these My brethren." This picture of contrasts is painted on a large canvas in Ezekiel 44, where the priests who went astray from God were restricted to ministering to the people and were prohibited from coming into God's Presence, while the sons of Zadok, who had remained faithful to God in the midst of Israel's apostasy, were invited to " '. . . come near to Me to minister to Me; and . . . stand before Me to offer to Me the fat and the blood,' says the Lord God" (Ezekiel 44:15). True worshippers of God are beckoned into His Presence to minister unto God Himself.

A third evidence of commendation is the promise " 'And He Who sits on the throne will dwell among them' " (Revelation 7:15). Not only are they invited before the Throne to minister directly to God, but God

177

pledges to live in their midst. They will know the Presence of God in their day-to-day activities. God will be the host in their homes, the partner in their businesses, and their companion at all times. This is harmonious with the loud voice John heard in heaven proclaiming, " 'Behold, the tabernacle of God is with men, and He will dwell with them, and they shall be His people, and God Himself will be with them and be their God' " (Revelation 21:3). God desired this in His relationship with Israel, but She refused it. It has been His unchanged desire throughout all the history of the world, and now that desire is being fulfilled in the lives of the true worshippers of God.

What follows is an outgrowth of the preceding provisions. " 'They shall neither hunger anymore nor thirst anymore; the sun shall not strike them, nor any heat,' " (Revelation 7:16). God protects His worshippers. Nothing from within or without can distress the one with whom God dwells. The psalmist taught this hundreds of years before John heard it from the elder in heaven. "He who dwells in the secret place of the Most High," the psalmist wrote, "shall abide under the shadow of the Almighty. I will say of the Lord, 'He is my refuge and my fortress . . .' Surely He shall deliver you from the snare of the fowler And from the perilous pestilence. . . . No evil shall befall you, Nor shall any plague come near your dwelling; For He shall give His angels charge over you, To keep you in all your ways" (Psalm 91:1-3, 10, 11). There is no protection like the protection God's Presence affords.

The fifth provision made for the worshipper is the shepherding care of the Lord. " 'For the Lamb who is in the midst of the throne will shepherd them' " (Revelation 7:17), the elder told John. David, who had learned to worship as a small lad while tending his father's sheep, understood the reality of God's shepherding, for he wrote, "The Lord is my shepherd; I shall not want" (Psalm 23:1). This psalm is probably the most familiar one in the entire Psalter, and its comfort has been drawn on by multitudes of people. It places the entire responsibility for our well-being upon God the Shepherd. He feeds, He leads, He restores, He removes fear, He anoints, and He extends goodness and mercy, for He is our Shepherd. Asaph connected shepherding with worship when he wrote, "So we, Your people and sheep of Your pasture, Will give You thanks forever; We will show forth Your praise to all generations" (Psalm 79:13). That's the way it is in heaven! That's the way it should be on earth!

Still another consignment given by God to worshippers is that " '. . . the Lamb who is in the midst of the throne will . . . lead them to living fountains of waters' " (Revelation 7:17). It was Jesus Himself Who spoke of fountains of living water when He was talking about worship with the woman at the well (John 4). He spoke of this again when "on the last day, the great day of the feast, Jesus stood and cried out, saying, 'If anyone thirsts, let him come to Me and drink. He who believes in Me, as the Scripture has said, out of his heart will flow rivers of living water.' But this He spoke concerning the Spirit, whom those believing in Him would receive; for the Holy Spirit was not yet given, because Jesus was not yet glorified" (John 7:37-39).

Using Jesus' definition of the Spirit being the fountain

of living water, this sixth commendation is a promise that God will consistently lead His worshippers to the flow of the Holy Spirit. What a pledge this is, for none of us can worship at an acceptable level except by the ministry of the Holy Spirit to and through us. Seasons of spiritual dryness can best be broken by coming before God's Presence in worship. He then will lead us to the freshness of the Spirit. Waiting for the exuberant overflow of the Holy Spirit before entering into the worship of God is like putting the cart before the horse. If we will worship, God will lead us to the living waters of the Spirit.

The seventh evidence of God's acceptance of the worship that was being so enthusiastically offered in heaven is the pledge " 'God will wipe away every tear from their eyes' " (Revelation 7:17). Sorrow ceases when worship begins. Isaiah knew this, for in speaking of the time when Israel "shall see the glory of the Lord, The excellency of our God," he wrote, "And the ransomed of the Lord shall return, And come to Zion with singing, With everlasting joy on their heads. They shall obtain joy and gladness, And sorrow and sighing shall flee away" (Isaiah 35:2, 10).

Sorrow and God's Presence do not go together. Sorrow may bring us to God's Presence, but as we worship in that Divine Presence, sorrow retreats and is replaced with the jubilant celebration of God that we have seen in the book of Revelation. As a matter of fact, one of the glorious provisions in the New Jerusalem is " 'God will wipe away every tear from their eyes; there shall be no more death, nor sorrow, nor crying; and there shall be no more pain, for the former things have passed away' " (Revelation 21:4). We may now live in the vale of tears, but worshippers transcend time and enter into the Presence of the God of eternity, where tears are wiped away and replaced with joy, singing, dancing, shouting, and pompom-waving.

"Blessing and honor and glory and power Be to Him who sits on the throne, And to the Lamb, forever and ever!" *Then the four living creatures said, "Amen!" And the twenty-four elders fell down and worshiped Him who lives* forever and ever.

"Amen! Blessing and glory and wisdom, Thanksgiving and honor and power and might, Be to our God forever and ever. *Amen."*

—Revelation 5:13, 14; 7:12
(emphasis added)

— 10 —

Worship Is Eternal

From antiquity comes the following story: "Over the triple doorway of the Cathedral of Milan there are three inscriptions spanning the splendid arches. Over one is carved a beautiful wreath of roses, and underneath is the legend 'All that pleases is but for a moment.' Over the other is sculptured a cross, and these are the words beneath: 'All that troubles is but for a moment.' But underneath the great central entrance in the main aisle is the inscription 'That only is important which is eternal.' "[1]

What a vast amount of our life is invested in activities and acquisitions that will not survive the test of the grave. We are such earth-bound creatures involved with time and space that eternal concepts seem almost foreign to us, even to Christians. Much of this is unavoidable and even essential, for our physical needs must be attended to, but many an aged person can retrospectively say with

---

[1] *The Speaker's Sourcebook*, compiled by Eleanor L. Doan. Grand Rapids, Michigan: Zondervan Publishing House, 1960, p. 96.

Solomon, " 'Vanity of vanities, all is vanity.' What profit has a man from all his labor In which he toils under the sun? One generation passes away, and another generation comes; But the earth abides forever" (Ecclesiastes 1:2-4).

TIME AND ETERNITY

The *philosophy* of eternity is still very indistinct in spite of the many generations of men who have grappled with it. Apparently we finite beings can form no positive idea of eternity. Even the Bible does not discuss time and eternity in any philosophical manner; it speaks of eternity in the practical sense of enhancing our confidence in God.

Probably the most common concept of eternity is endlessness, or time without end. Even in the popular language of the prophets, eternity was expressed in terms of time, although eternity is far above and beyond all limits of time.

Few persons can form a satisfactory concept of time, much less be able to comprehend eternity. What is time? It is likely that what a theologian or philosopher says of time will decidedly color his view of eternity. The great philosopher Aristotle said that time is the measure of motion, that bodies move through space, and the number of motion is time, but modern thinkers point out that the same motion can occur in different lengths of time, and these motions are often measured by something that is not an attribute of motion; so, brilliant though he was, Aristotle didn't correctly understand time, much less eternity, and neither do we.

It has been observed that Christian theologians usually pay little attention to the nature of time; hence their concepts of eternity are both incomplete and confused. Time and temporality are usually connected with change and motion. Things in time have a beginning, they develop in stages, and they come to an end. Since our concept of time is connected with change, time must have been created and must have a beginning. This actually makes time the antithesis of eternity, which has neither beginning nor end. Actually, when viewed in the absolute, eternity must be pronounced incommensurable with time.

Still, we earthlings, who are trapped in a time/space capsule, are unable to comprehend eternity without comparing it to and contrasting it with the dimension in which we live and die. Paul made this contrast in speaking of the seen and unseen: ". . . while we do not look at the things which are seen, but at the things which are not seen. For the things which are seen are temporary, but the things which are not seen are eternal" (2 Corinthians 4:18). Seen/unseen; temporary/eternal. That's a good beginning, but eternity is best conceived, not in the merely negative form of the non-temporal, or immeasurable time, but positively, as the mode of the timeless self-existence of Almighty God, for timeless existence—being or entity without change—is what we mean by eternity, and not mere everlastingness or permanence through time.

Since the days of Augustine and the Middle Ages, theologians have conceived of eternity as being an eternal "now"—the same definition they apply to God. Many have suggested that it was the introduction of sin, or the exercise of a will other than the will of God, that ushered in the dimension of time. Since we seem unable to think of eternity without intimately associating it with God, it is plausible to think that when sin separated the sinning one from God Almighty, it also expelled him from the dimension of eternity and incarcerated him in the prison of time. If this is so, eternity cannot return to mankind until sin is removed. Was it not access to the Tree of Life that Adam forfeited when he disobediently ate of the Tree of the Knowledge of Good and Evil? And was not his punishment death? Death to eternity—separation from God—expulsion from the garden—all were the consequences of forfeiting the rights to the Tree of Life. If eternity is the dimension of God, then time must be the dimension of those separated from God.

Since the acquisition of knowledge must proceed from the known to the unknown, isn't it probable that God would use time, in which we live, to be the basis for teaching us about eternity, in which we long to live? Time is less contradictory of eternity than it is helpful in revealing what we know of eternity; in that sense we might say that time is a parenthesis in eternity that gives us a picture, in type, of what eternity must be like.

Theologically we have been taught that we will continue in eternity what we have perfected in time; that is, the life we have received from God in time will be lived in God throughout all eternity. The worship we have entered into here in the temporal will continue in the eternal. We visualize the finalization of redemption releasing us from our time/space dimension into God's timeless/spaceless realm of reality. We don't know how to conceive of eternity apart from God.

GOD AND ETERNITY

The *essence* of eternity is God Himself. It is totally negative to speak of eternity as release from all time limits, although that is illustrative. The continuity of the temporal has its guaranty in the eternal, but while time is purely relative, eternity is not. Actually, contrasting time with eternity as an attempt to define eternity is doomed to failure from the start. The Scriptures develop the concept of eternity by consistently projecting God as an eternal Being, and the more we understand God, the better chance we have to understand eternity.

The Bible steadfastly teaches us that God is immutable —unchanging. Hebrews says, " 'You, Lord, in the beginning laid the foundation of the earth, And the heavens are the work of Your hands; They will perish, but You remain . . . they will be changed. But You are the same, And Your years will not fail' " (Hebrews 1:10-12). God must be immutable, for if He changed He would become either better or worse, and both are impossible for an absolutely perfect Being. To the prophet Malachi, God declared, " 'I am the Lord, I do not change' " (Malachi 3:6).

The immutability of God helps us understand eternity, for if God is unchangeable, if He has no beginning or end, we cannot conceive of Him existing in time, which is characterized by change. James refers to God as the "Father of lights, with whom there is no variation or shadow of turning" (James 1:17). If God is absolutely constant, there must be another mode of existence that characterizes and accommodates Him. Eternity becomes a necessity when we get a glimpse of the nature of God.

187

It was to the prophet Isaiah that the word came: "For thus says the High and Lofty One Who inhabits eternity, whose name is Holy: 'I dwell in the high and holy place, with him who has a contrite and humble spirit . . .' " (Isaiah 57:15), so God accommodates our theological need for a realm beyond time to be the abode of the immutable God by declaring that He does, indeed, inhabit eternity. God and eternity become inseparable when we realize that the God Who was never born cannot die, and that in declaring Him to be omniscient, we affirm that the Divine Mind is never ignorant of anything. God neither loses an idea He once had nor gains one He formerly did not know. There is no temporal succession in God's knowledge as we are accustomed to here in time.

It is far better to speak of God being the Eternal Deity rather than an eternal Now, for time is obviously not the form of God's life; that form is eternity, not as immeasurable time, but rather as a mode of being of the immutable God, Who, mercifully, is progressively revealing Himself in time.

Because man knows virtually nothing about the being of God, he naturally has an incomplete idea of eternity, but the Bible was written to give us a revelation of God, and, as a byproduct, a glimpse into eternity itself. Paul declared that "what may be known of God is manifest in them, for God has shown it to them. For since the creation of the world His invisible attributes are clearly seen, being understood by the things that are made, even His eternal power and Godhead, so that they are without excuse" (Romans 1:19, 20). God is the bridge between time and eternity, and He is the source of our revelation of eternity.

Throughout the Word, God is called "the Everlasting Father" (Isaiah 9:6), an "everlasting King" (Jeremiah 10:10), the "Creator, who is blessed forever" (Romans 1:25), and the One "who lives forever" (Daniel 12:7). It is said that He shall reign forever (*see* Micah 4:7), that His Word lives forever (*see* 1 Peter 1:23), that His salvation is an everlasting salvation (*see* Isaiah 45:17), and that He has loved us with an everlasting love (*see* Jeremiah 31:3). Everything that is connected with God, revealed in God, or ascribed to God is also connected with eternity, for eternity is part of the essential nature of God Himself.

In his final blessing on Israel, Moses linked the eternal God with perishable man by saying, " 'The eternal God is your refuge, And underneath are the everlasting arms' " (Deuteronomy 33:27), and at the Areopagus in Athens, Paul said of God, " '. . . He is not far from each one of us; for in Him we live and move and have our being . . .' " (Acts 17:27, 28). The Eternal God, knowing man's inability to invade eternity, chose to invade time and expose mankind to eternity.

CHRIST AND ETERNITY

Jesus Christ is the *extension* of eternity into time. John wrote, "No one has seen God at any time. The only begotten Son, who is in the bosom of the Father, He has declared Him" (John 1:18). The Greek word used for "declared" is *exegeomai*, meaning "to consider out loud, that is, to rehearse or unfold." One aspect of Jesus' revelation of the God of eternity was vocal—that is, rehearsing or unfolding the Godhead to mankind. He did this by demonstration, declaration, and display of the Divine nature. Since He was eternal God, He could honestly tell Philip, " 'He who has seen Me has seen the Father' " (John 14:9), and also tell the questioning Jews, " 'I and My Father are one' " (John 10:30).

Since eternity is part of the essential nature of God, when Jesus introduced the Father to us He also introduced us to eternity. To do so, "the Word became flesh and dwelt among us, and we beheld His glory, the glory as of the only begotten of the Father, full of grace and truth" (John 1:14). The eternal God condescended to become mortal man—temporal and time/space-limited —without losing His eternity, for although Jesus was very man of very man (as the theologians express it), He was equally very God of very God at all times.

The elders in heaven enthusiastically sang to Jesus, " 'For You . . . have redeemed us to God' " (Revelation 5:9), which includes being redeemed from mortality into immortality—from our realm into the realm of God Almighty. Unquestionably, the cross of Christ spanned from time to eternity— from earth to heaven. Christ Jesus came as the demonstrator and the distributor of eternal life, for John declared that "God has given us eternal life, and this life is in His Son. He who has the Son has life; he who does not have the Son of God does not have life" (1 John 5:11, 12).

Christ Jesus is the extension of eternity to mankind. He became a scale model of eternity in our time/space dimension, and He demonstrated eternal values on the scales of time. He made us aware of a life above and beyond our animal nature by speaking of heaven (and hell), angels, and principalities, and He generated a longing in us for this eternal life by giving us a taste of eternity in His association with us while He was on this earth.

Christ's claim to eternity and divinity was far too much for the religious rulers of the day, so they had Him crucified—little realizing that time cannot destroy eternity, that mortality cannot swallow up immortality any more than darkness can encompass light. "Up from the grave He arose, with a mighty triumph o'er His foes," we melodiously sing on Easter Sunday.[1] Christ Jesus, Who came as God's example of eternity, subsequently became our assurance of eternity, for in the presence of qualified witnesses He exchanged mortality for immortality by rising from the dead in a glorified [eternal] body. One of us mortals made it from time into eternity, and He assures us that we, in Him, can do the same, for He said, " 'Because I live, you will live also' " (John 14:19).

Paul spoke philosophically about this in his first letter to the church in Corinth when he wrote, "Now this I say, brethren, that flesh and blood cannot inherit the kingdom of God; nor does corruption inherit incorruption. Behold, I tell you a mystery: We shall not all sleep, but we shall all be changed—in a moment, in the twinkling of an eye, at the last trumpet. For the trumpet will sound, and the dead will be raised incorruptible, and we shall be changed. For this corruptible must put on incorruption, and this mortal must put on immortality. So when this corruptible has put on incorruption, and this mortal has put on immortality, then shall be brought to pass the saying that is written: 'Death is swallowed up in victory.'

---

[1] "Christ Arose," by Robert Lowery; all copyrights expired.

'O Death, where is your sting? O Hades, where is your victory?' The sting of death is sin, and the strength of sin is the law. But thanks be to God, who gives us the victory through our Lord Jesus Christ" (1 Corinthians 15:50-54).

"Victory through Christ!" Victory over time, which ends in death; victory unto eternity, which is endless life. Little wonder, then, that the residents of heaven worship Christ again and again. He is their link into eternity, and He is our entrance into eternal life. He is worthy of our unceasing worship as well.

ENTERING ETERNITY

Jesus Himself said, " 'I have come that they may have life, and that they may have it more abundantly' " (John 10:10), and in His high priestly prayer He added, " 'Father, the hour has come. Glorify Your Son, that Your Son also may glorify You, as You have given Him authority over all flesh, that He should give eternal life to as many as You have given Him. And this is eternal life, that they may know You, the only true God, and Jesus Christ whom You have sent' " (John 17:1-3).

Eternity is not invaded by persons, but persons can be invaded by eternity. Christ Jesus came to bring eternity to us in the here and now, and then, at some future time, to move us out of our space limitations into the fullness of eternity. The life that Christ gives to the repentant sinner is eternal life, for that is the only life that Christ possesses. Paul said this quite distinctly when he wrote, "For the wages of sin is death, but the gift of God is eternal life in Christ Jesus our Lord" (Romans 6:23). Eternity is more than a place; it is a form of life, and we mortals are invited to be participants in eternity by allowing the life of Christ to enter us while we are still in our time/space dimension.

Because we have so often equated eternity with heaven, many have lived their entire lives hoping to have eternal life after they die, without realizing that it is that eternal life which releases us from the space dimension at death. The Bible consistently teaches that we become possessors of eternal life upon our acceptance of Christ as our Savior, not at the moment of our death. We are actually given a bit of eternity to bring us into the full eternity of God. The fundamental difference between the believers in heaven and the Christians on the earth is location, not life. We have all been given eternal life, but they have their glorified eternal bodies and are in heaven, while we have that eternal life in our mortal bodies here on the earth.

Paul spoke of this change in life-source when he wrote, "I have been crucified with Christ; it is no longer I who live, but Christ lives in me; and the life which I now live in the flesh I live by faith in the Son of God, who loved me and gave Himself for me" (Galatians 2:20). In a very literal and actual sense, those who have the life of Christ within themselves also have touched eternity.

We enter eternity by an act of God, not by an act of our wills. It was God Who willed to save us unto Himself; the maximum contribution of an individual's will is to accept and respond to God's provision. Confession of sin and confession of Christ as Savior is our elementary part of entering into eternity. When our wills have surrendered to His will, God invades our lives with His life and introduces eternity within our spirits. From that point on, God's Spirit resides within our spirits to work out the plan of eternity in our lives. We discover that we "walk in the Spirit," are "led by the Spirit," and "live in the Spirit" (Galatians 5:16, 18, 25) while we are still residents of this earth. Salvation is a breakthrough into eternity for believers. We do not await it; we participate in it.

ETERNITY WITHIN US

It is probable that all of us are familiar with the classic passage in Solomon's writing which says, "To everything there is a season, A time for every purpose under heaven: A time to be born, and a time to die . . ." and so on (Ecclesiastes 3:1, 2). In the succeeding verses Solomon listed thirteen additional pairs of contrasted activities in life for which there is an appointed time. What we are less familiar with, however, is the statement which follows this poetic presentation of our limitation to time: "He [God] has made everything beautiful in its time. Also He has put eternity in their hearts" (Ecclesiastes 3:11). Solomon, by inspiration of the Holy Spirit, said that God has put man in time but eternity in man, and it is all beautiful.

"Eternity in their hearts." Of course! That is why we struggle so hard with our mortality and endeavor to break into eternity. There is something in our hearts that does not fit the limitation of our lives. We know that we have been made for something higher than this temporal world, but our inner instincts do not fit the rational picture of our environment any more than the dark earth fits the genetic strain of the tulip bulb. The life within the bulb will push itself through the surface of the soil into the air so that the true purpose of the plant might be seen in its beautiful flower. Similarly, we may be buried in time, but there is a working of eternity within us.

The desire for involvement with immortality is deep in the hearts of all persons. Many see their lives continuing into the future through their children and grandchildren. Others have tried to find endlessness through outstanding achievements in the arts and sciences. Egyptian kings sought it in the building of the pyramids, and others hoped that their memories would be held in perpetuity through the construction of palaces, cathedrals, or public gardens. All of these may extend a person's involvement with time, but none of them touches eternity. "The earth abides forever" (Ecclesiastes 1:4), Solomon said, but the scratches we put on its surface disappear with the blowing of the winds of change and the washing of the seas of time.

The apostle, the psalmist, and the prophet all affirmed that " 'All flesh is as grass, And all the glory of man as the flower of the grass. The grass withers, And its flower falls away, But the word of the Lord endures forever' " (1 Peter 1:24; *see* Psalm 103:15 and Isaiah 40:6-8). How fragile and fleeting is the allotted span of time any one person is permitted to occupy, and how frustrating this is, for there is the inner tug of eternity and the outer limitations of time. Since the cycle of man's days on the earth is often less than that of the wild beasts of the forest, God likens man to grass, which is seasonal and transient in nature.

Fragmentation is characteristic of life. We enter life knowing nothing, and all knowledge is acquired bit by bit. By the time anyone has accumulated sufficient knowledge and experience to be valuable, his life is snuffed out, much like blossoming clover is consumed by a herd of Jersey cows. Eternity may be in man's heart, but corruptible time is in his bloodstream.

There is, however, hope for fragile humanity. Christ Jesus came to overcome this continual fragmentation by sharing His eternal life with mortal creatures. He assures us that because He lived through the experience of death, we too can pass from time to eternity with continuity. He brought us from the inner desire for eternity to the actual experience of eternity, for in Him we are participants in eternity.

Our natural birth gave us a human nature and temporal life, but our new birth enabled us to have the nature of Christ, which is eternal in every aspect. We **have** eternal life when we have Christ Jesus. Because of this, we are assured that we are made for something better than a short life of threescore and ten years, and that this beautiful world is something better than a great grave.

However, for this very same reason we live with inner conflict. Part of our being is in the dimension of time, and part of our nature is already participating in eternity. Sometimes the conflict is as severe as crossing six or eight time zones: the mind relates to the local time of day, but the inner nature insists upon responding to the time to which it is accustomed at home, and no amount of logic can convince the stomach that it is time for dinner when it is programmed for breakfast.

Similarly, our spirit finds itself in conflict with the natural senses of the body: they constantly declare that we are limited to time, while the spirit is convinced that it must relate to eternity. The ensuing tug-of-war can make life a conflict of interests that discourages functioning well in either realm. Eternity becomes nebulous, while time becomes tedious. Like a college professor forced to earn his living as a dishwasher in a restaurant, life seems to have lost both purpose and fulfillment.

The Divine life which has been implanted in us must touch eternity in its function, or it will continually frustrate all avenues of life. It is imperative, then, that we learn how to function in eternity while we are still locked in time.

FUNCTIONING IN ETERNITY

If there is one thing which is eternal in its nature that we mortals can do while living in our time/space capsule, it is worship, for as surely as worship is inseparable from life on earth, worship is inseparable from eternity. Once we step from the limitations of time to the limitlessness of eternity, worship will be the central function of our existence. I do not mean that we will sit forever on a fleecy cloud with a harp and hymnal, for eternity will be filled with activity both here on this earth and in the New Jerusalem; perhaps the greatest contrast between the activity in time and the activity in eternity is that in eternity, everything we do will proceed out of worship and will likely be worship in its own right.

Here on earth, limited by time and space, we religiously involve ourselves in working *for* God. We visualize ourselves as His employees, and we seek to do His bidding throughout the world. A few who have come into an intimate fellowship with God have learned to minister *with* Him, but when our mortality has been stripped away, fully releasing us into eternity, we will minister exclusively *unto* God. As we see the angels respond to the bidding of God as an act of worship by doing it on God's behalf and for His pleasure, we too will begin to learn how to worship God in our deeds as well as in our declarations, and worship of God will replace mere work for God.

Worshippers of God break the time barrier and participate in eternity. They have an **eternal relationship,** for the Bible declares, "Beloved, now we are children of God; and it has not yet been revealed what we shall be, but we know that when He is revealed, we shall be like Him, for we shall see Him as He is" (1 John 3:2). Worshippers have learned to live in this eternal relationship, as is stated in the preceding chapter of this epistle of John: "If what you heard from the beginning abides in you, you also will abide in the Son and in the Father. And this is the promise that He has promised us—eternal life" (1 John 2:24, 25). It is the reception and retention of the Divine life—eternal life—that makes this eternal relationship possible.

Worship flows in an **eternal channel,** for worshippers "worship God in the Spirit, rejoice in Christ Jesus" (Philippians 3:3), and both the Spirit and Christ Jesus are declared to be eternal (*see* Hebrews 9:14 and 1 John 1:2). Not only is the object of our worship the eternal God, but the channel for the communication of that worship is the eternal Spirit; therefore, the act of worship involves the worshipper with eternity at its highest level: God Himself. With great understanding Augustine wrote, "Join thyself to the eternal God, and thou wilt be eternal."

Furthermore, worship is based on an **eternal redemption** (*see* Hebrews 9:12), and this redemption not only forms the basis of our worship but is often the theme and song of our worship. Again and again the heavenly residents include a thanksgiving for their redemption as an integral part of their worship. Redemption is an act of God that releases us from the slavery of sin, with its time/space limitation, into the freedom of sonship, with its inherent eternity.

It is self-evident that worship has as its exclusive object the **eternal God.** Nothing and no one short of God is ever an acceptable object for worship, so worship intimately involves the worshipper with eternity. In worship, God and the worshipper are united in the Divine realm of eternity, for John declared, " 'Behold, the tabernacle of God is with men, and He will dwell with them, and they shall be His people, and God Himself will be with them and be their God' " (Revelation 21:3). We need not await death or the Second Coming of Christ to enjoy the Presence of God or the flow of eternity; worship enables us to transcend time and space and to enter into the activities and associations of eternity while we still live here on this earth.

ETERNAL WORSHIP

The worship of the eternal God through His eternal Spirit is far more than merely touching eternity; it is actually entering into an activity that is eternal in every dimension. Worship has always been and shall always be. Worshippers reach from before the world until after the world and join the angels of heaven in worship and adoration of God, " 'the Alpha and the Omega, the

Beginning and the End . . . who is and who was and who is to come, the Almighty' " (Revelation 1:8).

When all the creatures in heaven, on the earth, under the earth, and in the sea are heard worshipping God, they declare, " 'Blessing and honor and glory and power Be to Him who sits on the throne, And to the Lamb, *forever and ever!*' " (Revelation 5:13, emphasis added), and later the angels, elders and living creatures fall on their faces before the Throne and worship God, saying, " 'Amen! Blessing and glory and wisdom, Thanksgiving and honor and power and might, Be to our God *forever and ever.* Amen' " (Revelation 7:12, emphasis added). Worship will not be a one-time act upon our entrance into heaven; worship will be as eternal as the object of our adoration.

Thank God that all of the elements that go to make up worship have been made available to us in the here and now so that when we reach the "sweet by and by," we will already be comfortable with worship. How glorious it will be when we join that great worshipping throng in heaven without fear, embarrassment, or disqualification because we're already on familiar ground. The Spirit of the Lord is now preparing the Church for Her eternal activity by bringing us into worship in our present relationship with God.

God has provided everything that is essential in order for us to worship Him in spirit and in truth. That is His move toward us. It is now up to the individual believer to apply each of these provided elements of worship in his own life in order to be a true worshipper of God. The next move is ours!

Other books by Judson Cornwall:

Freeway Under Construction	$ .95
Give Me—Make Me	1.25
Let Us Abide	4.95
Let Us Be Holy	4.95
Let Us Draw Near	4.95
Let Us Enjoy Forgiveness	4.95
Let Us Praise	4.95
Let Us See Jesus	4.95
Let Us Worship	4.95
Profiles of a Leader	4.95

By Judson and Thomas Cornwall:

Please Accept Me	4.95

Order from
Christian Books International
2500 Hamilton Blvd.
South Plainfield, NJ 07080
(Add $1.00 for mail orders)